HORSES

Around My Heart

*This book is dedicated to the loving memory of my
parents, Harold and Muriel Kennedy, and to my husband
of more than 42 years who never could quite share my
love of horses yet he understood it and encoraged me. And
to our children, Heather, Terry Lee, and Roderick, and to
their children who continue to make me proud of them.*

*Dr. Keith Degenhardt gets a wet kiss from one of the
Gango Drinkers of the Wind.*

HORSES
Around My Heart

by
Mary Burpee

Borealis Press Ltd.
Ottawa, Canada
2004

Canadä

*The Publishers acknowledge the financial assistance
of the Government of Canada through the Book Publishing
Industry Development Program (BPIDP)
for our publishing activities*

National Library of Canada Cataloguing in Publication Data

Burpee, Mary (Kennedy), 1918-
    Horses around my heart / Mary Burpee.

ISBN 0-88887-189-9

    1. Burpee, Mary (Kennedy), 1918- 2. Horses—Canada—
Anecdotes. 3. Horsemen and horsewomen—Canada—Biography.
I. Title.

SF301.B87 2003   636.1'0092   C2003-902260-9

Cover design by Bull's Eye Design, Ottawa.
Typesetting by Chisholm Communications, Ottawa.
Photographs by Mary Burpee and others.

Printed and bound in Canada on acid-free paper

Table of Contents

Chapters

Chapter One

A Three-Way Race

The moon was a ghostly galleon tossed upon stormy seas. The road was a ribbon of moonlight over the purple moor. But no highwayman travelled that road. Instead a dark-cloaked figure, a crouching spectre on a jet-black stallion galloped like the wind through shadowy glens, dodged bold-fisted rocks dappled in moonlight, slipped wraith-like between towering trees, floated eerily over blackthorn hedges.

Do I carry the gene of that long-dead highwayman? A swashbuckling rascal who charmed the ladies even while he was relieving them of their jewels, and had gentlemen coveting the animal he rode more than they mourned the loss of their watches and their purses?

Why couldn't I? I carry the genes of a sea captain who commanded the Prince of Orange's flag ship back when every sea captain worth his salt did a bit of pirating for Jolly Olde England whenever the opportunity presented itself. That ancestor is spoken of with pride and respect, but if there's a highwayman who valued his horse more than he valued his life, he's a well-kept secret in the murky recesses of the family closet of best-forgotten skeletons.

But if not from my genes, then where did I really get the love of horses that has shaped, and sometimes dominated, my life?

Most likely it was fostered by something my father retold with pride every year on April 6 for 56 years. That something was the story of a race between a black horse, a new Buick car, and a hurrying stork. The horse won.

1

My entry into this world wasn't to be in a sterile hospital ward, but in a homesteader's two-room shack on Section 28-41-7 W 4th in the very young province of Alberta. Harold Kennedy, remembering his son's difficult entry into the world two and a half years earlier, was determined this time his wife must have a doctor *and* a midwife in attendance.

He had it all planned. At the first indication of labour he would hitch up the buggy, drive the four and a half miles to Hughenden, call the doctor, then quickly head back home, stopping on the way to pick up the midwife whom he would have alerted on his way into town.

The dawn chorus of April birds hadn't yet started their warm-up twitter when Harold Kennedy leaped out of bed as if the tails of his nightshirt had caught fire.

"Hold on, girl. I'll get Doc Ferguson and Mrs. Groves, and be back as fast as I can." Kennedy was hastily pulling on his pants as he spoke.

"Do be careful, dear. You know how Darky loves to ru ..." The words trailed into a gasp as another spasm of pain swept through the young woman's swollen body.

Harold Kennedy was in the barn, throwing the driving harness on a lanky black horse almost before his wife finished speaking. The memory of the ordeal she'd gone through birthing their son was a compelling urgency that sprouted wings on his steel-toed work boots.

His own excitement fuelled the blacks. The buggy careened out of the yard behind flying hooves that needed no urging. It took the turn from the gate on two wheels, then righted itself to hurtle down the trail. Metal tires struck sparks ricocheting off stones which had gone unnoticed by the slow-moving ox-wagons that had first cut these meandering ruts ribboning the prairie.

After three miles the buggy was momentarily slowed to negotiate the narrow gate leading to the Groves' homestead, then whirled on up to the house where a terse message was shouted through a partially open window. "Mrs. Groves! I'll pick you up as soon as I call Doc Ferguson and then get back here. Be ready!"

Then Darky was off again in a rising cloud of dust. With still two miles to go. Kennedy prayed the doctor was in. If he wasn't... ? Kennedy couldn't let his mind dwell on that possibility. Worry lines dominated his grey face. He gave a low peremptory whistle to a horse already running with every inch of his body.

The young man stopped in Hughenden just long enough to satisfy himself that the doctor was awake and dragging on his trousers, then the buggy was rocketing up the road again. Cresting Allan's hill Kennedy looked back, saw the doctor's new Buick leaving town, and felt a wave of intense relief wash over him. With less than a mile separating car and buggy, his rig would almost certainly be overtaken before he stopped for the midwife.

Kennedy knew Darky had a "thing" about allowing another rig to pass him. He also knew the horse had a hatred, bordering on fear, of motor cars, and now the wild glitter in the black's eyes, his laid-back ears, the long striding legs reaching farther, always still farther, their tempo steadily increasing, made it clear he was running with purposeful intent. No noisy, smelly, puffing tin-lizzy was going to pass him. Not if he could help it.

Although Kennedy was aware of the hostility, verging on panic, that took possession of Darky whenever he saw a car, it had never been of much concern to him. In 1918 it was rare to see a motor car, especially on prairie trails such as this, trails cut by ox-carts and lumber wagons.

The young man was much too concerned about his wife to let anything like that bother him now. If the black wanted to run, more power to him.

When Kennedy, leaving the Groves' yard, realized the Buick, which was now cresting Allan's hill, hadn't gained on him despite his stop for the midwife, his whole body tingled. He felt the same devil-take-the-hindmost excitement he had felt as a boy in Ireland when their yacht had flaunted its canvas at the prows of larger, more pretentious sailing vessels. Gripping the lines, he steadied the horse into the turn, then, out on the road again he let out a lusty cheer, half encouragement, half defiance.

Mrs. Groves, sitting ramrod straight and just as rigid, clutched her over-sized hat with one white-knuckled hand, the seat railing with the other, her eyes fixed in horror on the racing horse. Her face was a mask of terror; her mouth worked as if to form words, yet no words came out. She had been stricken dumb by the thought that she was much too young to die. Only her lips could move and they were mouthing silent, hurried prayers. But Heaven better be quick, or it would be too late. Her in-drawn hiss of breath sounded louder in her own ears than even the pounding of hooves in front of her.

Mrs. Groves was convinced the foam-flecked monster between the shafts was a devil in disguise. So why was Kennedy wrapped in a beatific glow?

Finally the heaving horse was pulled to a stop in the Kennedy yard, and Mrs. Groves, still clutching her hat and mouthing prayers, was unceremoniously hustled into the house.

Kennedy had Darky unhitched and in the barn when the doctor's car chugged noisily into the yard. Cooling the horse, caring for him, would have to wait.

Kennedy needed to check on the woman who meant more to him than life itself.

Whether it was an inherited gene or the repetition of that story, told every April 6 for 56 years, the love of horses and riding that began as a small child is still with me. So it seems appropriate that I should write about the many special horses who have wound themselves around my heart.

Chapter Two

Darky—Fantasy and Fact

Darky's hatred of cars wasn't his only quirk. He considered it a duty to chase strange horses and small children out of his pasture. He did this with such enthusiasm that I'd almost rather talk back to God than go into the pasture when Darky was in it.

"Hey! Mary! D'ya wanna come with me to get the cows?" The words had a careless ring. Yet there was something about them that hinted my six-year-old brother might be more anxious to have me go with him than he cared to admit. I had been playing "horse." Which meant I was galloping around the yard holding a length of binder twine looped over one foot. That was the bridle to control my wild mustang.

"No, Jimmy. I'm scared Darky'll chase us." Having said that I gave the string attached to my foot a "get-going" twitch and galloped away on my pretend mount.

"He can't chase us, Stupid. He's in the barn." My brother, two and a half years my senior, watched me a moment, then added in a voice ringed with disgust. "No one but a dumb girl would tie a string around her foot and think it was a saddle horse." There was such derision in his voice I stopped and snarled defensively.

"I *am not* stupid. I know a string on my foot doesn't make it a horse. It's only pretend." My voice was stiff with wounded dignity. Then I added in a conciliatory manner. "If you're sure Darky isn't in the pasture I'll go with you. Provided you'll help me look for bluebells for Mom. Maybe there'll be shooting-stars out now too."

Jim's grunt passed for a promise. Hand in hand we skipped off to find the cows, confident there would be

7

no twelve hundred pounds of black fury streaking towards us this evening.

Dad had no explanation for why a gelding who never flicked an ear at us when saddled or in harness should become so possessive of his pasture that he felt obliged to drive out all intruders. Even if they happened to be his owner's small children. Nor did Dad believe Darky would actually hurt us. Although the horse certainly looked dangerous enough to startle rattlesnakes.

But Mom, remembering how Darky's teeth had slashed the rump of a new horse, and then run the frightened animal into a barbed wire fence, wasn't so sure. She was constantly warning us, "Stay away from Darky."

She could have saved her breath. I'd face fire-eating dragons rather than risk having Darky chase me. So I stayed out of the pasture when he was loose. Which wasn't often.

Pasture privileges were rare for a horse who was Dad's driver for trips to town, his saddle horse when cattle on open ranges had strayed too far and needed to be found and brought closer to home. The rest of the time Darky was teamed with Beauty, a good-looking Clydesdale mare. This pair, together with the greys Ray and Rowdy, were Dad's hard-working farm horses when I was small.

As the milk cows straggled homeward Jim and I darted about picking the bluebells that hid in shy profusion amid lush grass growing in a moist draw between two sloughs. Then we hurried to catch up with our dawdling charges. The cows had almost reached the corral where a small smudge fire would offer them relief from the torment of mosquitoes, when they broke into a run. My frightened scream "Darky's out! He's coming for us!" had startled them. As it had a flock of crows that arose now en masse from a poplar bush to flap into the sunset like black-hooded hangmen.

I was already racing for the fence with winged terror in my feet when Jim's shout "Run Mary! Run! Quick! Crawl under the wires!" caught up with me. My brother stopped long enough to snatch up a convenient stick, then followed, brandishing it over his shoulder in what I suppose he hoped was a threatening manner.

A black horse, having just rolled and shaken the dust from his sweat-streaked hide, was snorting up out of a dry gulch. When he saw us, he half-reared, then came for us at a booming gallop, snaking his head in the way of wild stallions herding their harem. The low-slung head, the outstretched neck, the ears laid flat back, the wicked glitter in his eyes sent fear skipping up my back. Blood rushing through my veins pounded in my ears as we raced towards the fence. It wasn't far. But could we reach it in time?

The ground was hard and unyielding as I half-rolled, half-tumbled under the bottom wire. Jimmy, still brandishing the stick, was right behind me. As soon as we were out of Darky's reach, the fire went out of the horse like air from a pricked balloon. He slammed to a stop, nibbled a bit of grass, then, frisking and bucking, whirled and raced back to his teammates.

That, my first actual memory of Darky, makes it hard to give credence to my next one-on-one encounter with him, which must have happened a year later, because by this time there was a school pony in our pasture.

Dad had often swung me up onto Darky's saddle so I could ride with him to the barn. And I had no fear of any horse in harness. Yet the sound of horses galloping in from the pasture always sent me racing for the safety of the house-yard. Darky had trained me well.

Sometimes I mistook the drumming of a bush partridge for pounding hooves, but today there was no mistake. The horses were coming.

I ran to the doorstep and climbed up on Dolly Grey, a rocking-horse with real mane and tail and a removable saddle. Dad had bought her in Chicago for Jim. But it seems I had taken possession of her before I was old enough to walk, rocking her back and forth in the middle of the kitchen floor until it would have driven anyone but a mother to distraction. Even now, at the age of five, I still rode her. She stood as high as a St. Bernard dog.

I stopped rounding up imaginary steers to watch Darky and the other horses gallop in from the pasture. Soon Darky was trying to reach a big clump of green grass on my side of the fence, and not having much success. Sliding off Dolly Grey, I edged closer.

Instead of backing away at my approach or snaking his head over the fence to try and bite me, as I had half expected, Darky's ears pricked forwards.

A sort of reckless bravado replaced caution. I pulled the grass and held it out to him with my heart hammering in my ears. My knees suddenly felt as if they were stuffed with feathers and in danger of collapsing. I was tempted to throw the grass in his face and run.

Darky's ebony neck arched a little. He watched me a moment from eyes white-ringed with suspicion. Then, as if having reached a satisfactory decision, he blew softly, reached out his velvet muzzle and took the grass as gently as a duchess fingers her finest crystal.

Wow! Emboldened, I pulled more grass, and Darky followed me around the perimeter of the fence waiting for each of my small offerings.

Hey! I think he likes me. Maybe I can touch his halter. No sooner the thought than a small hand shot out and caught hold of his halter. I had expected him to throw up his head and jerk away from me as our school pony, Toby, always did.

Darky didn't fling up his head. Instead, he lowered it so I could pet his chocolate-brown muzzle, feel its velvety softness. Sheer delight prickled my skin, made me forget to be scared.

The next moment I had crawled under the fence and was at Darky's shoulder, reaching to pat the glossy crest of his neck, running my fingers through his mane. He seemed to like it. I beamed like an idiot.

Needing to share my new-found bravery with someone, I led Darky around to the kitchen window, yelling "Hey Mom! Come and look. I can lead Darky." It was the greatest moment of my young life.

I was never afraid of Darky again. Now when he came trotting up to me it was for the treat I often sneaked for him. He became my favourite horse. And I liked to think I was special to him too.

If he did something clever, like pushing the pump handle up and down with his head when the water trough was empty, I felt as proud as the parent of a precocious child. It wasn't so good when he learned how to open the oat-bin door. That could have killed him as well as all the other horses. Dad had to immediately put Darky-proof latches on all the granary doors.

If Darky was in disgrace I suffered with him. It was when Darky got himself in my father's bad books by running a new horse into the fence, and was shut in the barn without food and sometimes even beaten for his misdemeanours, that I ached for him. Dad might as well have spanked me and sent me supperless to bed.

I'd probably have actually suffered with Darky if Dad had known what I'd been up too. I'd watch my chance to sneak in through a barn window to bring the black a treat. It might be a bundle of green grass I'd pulled or hay dug from the stack. If Mom wasn't in the kitchen there might even be an apple hidden in my pocket.

Then I'd run a small hand over his silky hide, whispering, "It really isn't your fault if the new horse won't stay away from fences. But please, Darky, next time don't chase it. Then Dad can't blame you if it gets cut up."

Darky would munch contentedly, sometimes turning his face to mine, as if giving a softly blown promise that in the future he'd mend his ways. But he never did. He was so over-possessive of his own pasture he'd try to run every new horse Dad bought out of his territory. Just as he had once done with kids.

Darky was a lanky, rough-coupled black of uncertain lineage. But somewhere in his background there must have been an infusion of Arabian blood to give him the stamina and that special something few other breeds possess.

He could work all week on the plough, but when turned out on Saturday evening he still had enough energy to try to chase away any new horse he saw in his pasture. It didn't matter if he had worked alongside that horse all week and shared a stall with it at night. It was seeing the horse in his pasture for the first time that goaded him into trying to drive it out. It got so Dad hated to bring in a new horse because of Darky.

Yet Dad liked him. In addition to doing field work he was our stylishly turned-out driver, and Dad's stock horse that few of the locals could outclass on the fall roundups. In the eyes of one small girl he was perfection. Even when he broke the neck of a three-year-old steer.

That steer, summering on the open range, had grown as wild as proverbial sin. Come fall, Dad decided the only way to get it home was to rope it and snub it to the saddle horn. Darky dragged it for five long fighting miles.

When the home corrals were close, Dad got off to open a gate. He stood to one side waiting for Darky and the steer to walk through. Then he'd close it behind them. Darky went through. The steer didn't. It ran to the opposite side of the gatepost.

The post became a fulcrum. Now each step the horse took tightened the rope around the animal's neck still more. There was no way the steer could turn and go through the gate properly unless the rope slackened off, and Darky had no intention of allowing that to happen. He'd been pulling the critter all day. There seemed no reason to stop now, when home and oats were in sight, just because Dad was yelling "Whoa Darky! Whoa!"

Before Dad could get to him and loosen the rope the critter's neck had snapped.

Darky didn't get blamed for that episode. But there were fresh steaks on the table the next day.

If the bank manager's young son hadn't died, and if I hadn't been fighting the same type of mastoid infection, I might never have been able to call Darky mine.

When a new Atwater Kent radio, bringing the magic of Fibber McGee and Molly, Amos and Andy, the Lux Theatre and the Farmer into our home, couldn't stir up even a flicker of interest in my eyes, Dad racked his brain for something that would.

He sat beside my bed one morning, his cold-reddened hands holding the can of Old Chum pipe tobacco that was almost the same colour blue as the smoke that curled around his head. "Mary, your mother and I are wondering what you would like for Christmas."

My answer shot out with a speed that astounded him. "Darky."

"But Mary dear, we can't give you Darky. Daddy needs him. And what if Jim and Eileen both want a horse too?" Mom's logic, as always, was irrefutable, but I paid it no attention.

"Your Mother's right, Mavourneen. Darky's not a horse you can ride. Better think of something else."

"There isn't *anything* I want ... except Darky." The words were like tears.

Dad stroked my hair thoughtfully, pipe clenched firmly in his teeth.

Finally he spoke, and his voice had a businesslike ring. "If your mother and I give you Darky to call your own you must understand I'll have to use him just as I've always done. And there'll be no riding him until I say so. Agreed?"

I'd have agreed to eat live toads for the right to call Darky mine. Dad and I shook hands solemnly. I owned my first horse. It didn't matter that it was in name only.

Whether it was the thrill of being able to call Darky mine or a visit to an Edmonton ear specialist that cured my mastoid infection is open to speculation. But soon after Christmas I went back to school.

After missing so much it seemed I would never get caught up with the rest of my class. School, especially anything to do with arithmetic, became an ordeal. And the long golden ringlets Mom said were my crowning glory didn't help. They were more like a crown of thorns. I hated them. They made me different from every other girl in school at a time when I wanted to look exactly like them.

However, Mom said, "Girls with bobbed hair all look the same. It's so common." I'd have died to look common. But dying doesn't come that easy. So I had to suffer each night while Mom frowned and said through lips pursed in concentration, "Mary, for goodness' sakes child! Stand still. Don't fidget so. It'll only take longer."

"But Mom," I'd wail. "You put in so many curler-rags I can't sleep. They make my head all lumpy."

My mother wasn't one to easily lower her standards. Her mouth would set in an unyielding line as she said quietly, "You'll get used to sleeping with curlers, Sweet-heart. I did when I was your age." She was determined her daughter must start the day looking genteel. It wouldn't last, of course. Soon enough the carefully brushed ringlets turned into a rat's-nest of snarls that worsened as the day progressed.

However, being self-conscious about my long hair made me unusually shy. When I wanted to look exactly like all my friends I stood out like a Spanish onion in a fruit bowl. So I shrank deeper into my shell and dreamed impossible dreams.

Darky turned into a superhorse, a Pegasus who would always come thundering to my rescue. In my day-dreams I would defy the teacher in a way every school kid has dreamed of doing. "No, Mr. Roberts, I won't throw out my gum. And I don't intend to stand up and recite memory work. Not ever again. So put that in your pipe and smoke it." Or "I don't feel like going to the blackboard to do arithmetic problems today. If you're so smart, do them yourself."

While I was dropping these bombshells every kid in the room would be staring in wide-eyed disbelief, envi-ous, but knowing they could never hope to match the sheer hellery of my aplomb.

I might cast a cold, vaguely condescending smile on a teacher whose mouth would be opening and closing with nothing coming out except the sound of maniacal breath rasping in his throat. If he groped wildly in his desk drawer for the strap, his purple face so like an over-inflated balloon, I'd titter a little and aim a carrying whisper to the boy in the front desk. "Better duck, Harvey. He's going to burst."

Having said that I'd sweep out of the classroom with all the hauteur of an imperial duchess, tossing carelessly back over my shoulder. "Ta-ta, Mr. Roberts. I really must be going. My horse has arrived."

Then with an Errol Flynn leap I'd land on the back of a rearing horse whose flailing hooves and bared teeth were sending clear warnings to anyone foolhardy enough to think they could harm his mistress.

Half-hidden by whipping mane and plumed tail, I'd crouch low on Darky's back as he galloped away, clearing the school fence as if it had been a length of string tossed carelessly onto the ground.

Every pair of eyes in the school would follow me in a mixture of awe and envy until Darky had whirled out of sight in a cloud of dust. Then Mr. Roberts, looking as if he'd been kicked in the stomach by a mule, would drag the class back to the humdrum reality of chalk and blackboards with a bellow that would cower a rhino.

Of course Darky and I always performed some superman humanitarian feat before the next school day rolled around. A feat that couldn't fail to win us the admiration and respect of the entire community. Even Mr. Roberts would feel obliged to grudgingly compliment me in front of the entire class.

Good old Darky. A little girl dreamed impossible dreams but he kept his feet firmly on the ground, accepting my love and a stall mucked out so enthusiastically that Dad sometimes complained I was putting too much "clean straw" on the manure wagon.

Dad liked Beauty, Darky's regular teammate, well enough. But I had serious doubts about her. She couldn't find even one foal in our pasture. Yet Albert Gans's mares found them every spring in his pasture just across the road. Obviously Beauty wasn't looking hard enough. Mom had said, "Cows and mares find their babies in the pasture," so I periodically tramped through poplar bluffs and other shady places hoping to find the foal Beauty had missed. But I didn't have any luck either.

Chapter Three

Toby

Even before I lost my fear of Darky another horse had come into my life.

"Sweetheart, Daddy brought a new pony home this morning. His name is Toby. He's for Jimmy to ride to school just as soon as the weather warms up. Would you like to go out now and ride him? You'll have to dress warmly."

It must have been Mom's concern over my "nothing to do" listlessness following a bout with the measles that caused such an out-of-character remark. Normally she was the very soul of caution. My mother would never have encouraged a five-year-old to ride a pony, even one sold as "child-safe," until satisfied it had been properly tried and tested. Not even her hope that March winds and sun could restore colour to her child's cheeks and bounce to her soul would normally have caused such an indiscretion.

"You mean I can be the *first* to ride Toby, Mom? Even before Jimmy gets to? Wow!" I suddenly felt more grown-up than I had felt in my entire five years.

"I don't see why not, dear." Mom allowed herself a cultured sigh. Jim, her first-born, showed no interest in horses. In fact she had doubts he would adapt to riding at all. Four and a half miles every morning and again after school seemed too far for a boy who wouldn't be eight until September, and who didn't like riding.

Yet when she had voiced that concern to her husband his reply had been unusually brusque. "Other boys his age are riding. I don't intend to pamper our son. Besides, when spring comes the farming will get behind if I have to stop and make two trips to school every day. If James doesn't want to ride he can take the buggy."

Having said that, Dad's most immediate concern seemed to be the business of tamping tobacco into his pipe. When that was accomplished he struck a match on the seat of his overalls (an accomplishment that elevated him to magician status in my eyes) and went out.

Mom's mouth had clamped shut and there was a red spot coming and going on either cheek, the way it sometimes does when we kids have tried her patience almost to the spanking point.

Of the two alternatives she had hoped riding would be her son's choice. But how to get the boy interested? Perhaps if Jim saw his little sister riding a new pony he'd want to try it. Mom hoped so.

I had been riding Dolly Grey since the toddler age, rocking endlessly back and forth, my eyes on a picture that hung on our kitchen wall just above the table. It was a rustic scene of cattle being driven along a treed path in the Highlands of Scotland, and it fired my imagination. I'd rock wildly back and forth on Dolly Grey, shouting "Hi! Hi!" in such a monotonous imitation of Dad chasing cattle on Darky that anyone but a mother would have gagged me. Yet Mom hadn't seen any of my enthusiasm for riding Dolly Grey rubbing off on her son.

Now she sighed and allowed herself a quick memory of her carefree life at Brackenfell, the stately English mansion that had once been home. Then her chin elevated in stiff acceptance and she dragged her thoughts back to where I was already pulling on a sweater.

"Daddy says Toby seems very quiet. Wear your high felt boots and your old coat. Come on. I'll tie a scarf around your toque. We don't want you getting earache again.

"Daddy's at the barn. He'll help you bridle Toby and give you a leg up. Have a nice ride, dear. But be careful."

Her mother instinct made that cautionary warning a must even though the pony her husband had brought home was so emaciated it seemed improbable he could go faster than a walk ... even with a pushing wind.

Now her eyes went to the window where she could see me riding Toby in slow plodding circles around the yard, looking as secure on his back as a bur on a wool sock.

"Did you enjoy your ride, dear?" Mom was helping me pull off my felt boots as she spoke.

"Sure did, Mom. Afterwards I took Toby's bridle off. All by myself. Daddy said I did real good. You know something? Toby's going to be my favourite horse." I had more optimism than good judgement.

"That's nice, dear."

Later she said, "Would you like to ride Toby again this afternoon? You could take him to meet Daddy when he comes back from picking Jimmy up at school."

There was something in the questioning look Dad shot her from across the dinner table that made Mom add quickly. "Or would you rather go with Daddy and Darky in the cutter?"

"Hmm." I chewed thoughtfully. This was a serious choice. It was always exciting to go with Dad when he drove Darky.... Besides, Dad always told me stories about his boyhood in Ireland, about the pranks he and his brothers pulled on their teachers.

Mom said the Kennedy boys must have been a terrible trial to their teachers. And she felt sorry for them. The teachers, that is.

Finally I looked up. "I think I'll go in the cutter with you, Daddy. That way I can be first to tell Jimmy about Toby."

"Good choice." Harold Kennedy, spooning a liberal helping of rice pudding and stewed prunes onto his plate, didn't think this was the time to tell his wife he hadn't entirely approved of her suggestion that their child ride an untried horse. Not out on the road. He wanted to know more about the animal first. The pony did look more dead than alive, but still ... you never know.

In the months that followed Jimmy did ride Toby to school and got along well enough with him. It was the weekends I lived for. Then I could ride the bay pony around the yard and up the hill to the letter-box, a covered box nailed to the gate-post for the convenience of neighbours bringing Kennedy mail out from town.

As Toby's bay coat grew glossy and his ribs disappeared beneath layers of fat, behavioural quirks developed that hadn't been apparent in the half-starved pony Dad brought home in March.

Now, when turned out to pasture he became hard to catch. Instead of keeping his head in the oat bucket long enough for a child to snap a lead-rope onto his halter, he'd snatch a mouthful of grain and quickly back away. If I caught hold of his halter he'd fling up his head and jerk away.

However, when he did allow himself to get caught, he didn't really object to galloping on the level or even up the hill to the mailbox. But he did it with such a total lack of enthusiasm it was obvious he considered anything faster than a walk, or at best a trot, to be a needless waste of energy.

Yet whenever I booted him into a downhill gallop I knew I'd get bucked off at the bottom of the hill alongside the three big rocks that hadn't yet been hauled away. Invariably if Toby galloped down that hill he'd stop at the bottom and buck. Just as invariably I'd fall off. I never rode out one of his bucking spells. Neither did I give up trying.

The possibility I might be thrown onto a rock never bothered me much. But it was terribly important that my parents not see me getting dumped, because if they did I'd be grounded. "Until you're older." Which might be a week, a month ... even a year if Mom was issuing the grounding edict. That loomed as a lifetime of grey, dismal nothing-to-do days stretching to eternity.

Dad's ultimatum "No riding until you're older, Mavourneen" I could usually get annulled within a few days by reasoning "but I *am* older now, Daddy." Whereas Mom's sentences were for real. When she said "the rest of the holidays," "six months," "a year," she meant it.

While getting bucked off never bothered me, being grounded did. So after I was allowed to ride again I really would make a conscientious effort not to gallop Toby down a hill. But eventually the daredevil on my shoulder would begin taunting again "Make him gallop. You'll stick with him this time." And Toby would be whacked into a downhill gallop ... a gallop that always ended with the same results.

Mom could never understand why anyone who fell off a horse as often as I did could like riding. "When she fell off today, Harold, I expected the child to come in crying, so sore she'd be glad to play with her dolls, but do you know what the little rascal did? She jumped up, ran after Toby and caught him, led him over to the wagon wheel, and the next second she had climbed back on and was flying off across the field again. Really, dear, I don't know what we're going to do with that child. If she keeps it up she'll kill herself."

Harold Kennedy stroked his wife's dark hair thoughtfully. "I don't think we need worry too much, Girl. Not when she rides bareback. A straight tumble isn't apt to do her much harm. Not like getting a foot caught in a stirrup and being dragged."

When winter's snow and cold put an end to field work Dad drove Jim to school with Darky in the morning. In the afternoon the boy was expected to start walking home. Some days he might walk a mile, even two, before the cutter met him. If the afternoon was mild and Dad was trying to get extra straw or hay hauled into the feed yard (or maybe it was time to start cleaning next spring's seed grain), Mom would hitch Toby to the cutter, bundle me and eighteen-month-old Eileen in beside her, and we'd set out to meet Jim.

Our dog Tidge had long ago decided Mom was his special responsibility. Wherever she went he went too. Tidge was a short-haired bird dog boasting better breeding, I expect, than most of the farm dogs of his day. But despite his lineage he was no beauty. And he smelt worse than a barrel of rotten skunks.

Tidge had a problem. He had mange. Insidious and debilitating mange.

No matter how faithfully Mom wrestled the big red-brown dog into a bath reeking of creosol, then smeared him with a still more vile-smelling concoction reputed to cure mange, he continued to scratch. He scratched until his hair came off in great slabs exposing raw, ugly scabs that oozed and bled. And still he scratched.

Our parents warned us not to play with Tidge. We might get mange. They could have saved their breath. Nothing, short of perhaps the threat of instant death, would have induced me to play with a dog that stank like Tidge.

Indeed, if Tidge had been an ordinary farm dog Dad would probably have disposed of him in a humane fashion long ago. But because Tidge had been given them by a special friend, Mom was determined to do her best by the dog. And the dog reciprocated by lavishing her with his unlimited love and affection.

Toby, despite his other quirks, was a fast learner. Especially if it meant saving himself some effort. He knew that as soon as the cutter reached the boy walking towards it, he could turn around and head for home. There seemed no reason to waste any time in doing it.

It might have been the team and sleigh that hove into view just before Mom reached Jim that made her start to turn Toby when she did. Perhaps in her hurry to get turned and on her way before the team reached her she neglected her husband's warning, "Watch Toby when you're turning. He's apt to try to pivot too short and upset the cutter."

Those words came flashing back now. But they came too late. The cutter upset, dumping Mom, Eileen, and me out into the snow to kick and sprawl our way out of a tangled confusion of blankets, foot-warmer, and dog.

It only took a moment for me to wriggle free and get up. Mom wasn't so lucky. Eileen was a dead weight across her legs. Tidge, thinking he ought to do something, was straddling his beloved mistress, licking her face with a determination both stoic and dedicated ... as if that would surely put everything to rights again. The more Mom tried to shove Tidge away the faster he licked.

Eileen seemed as lifeless as a lump of petrified coal ... except for her vocal cords. They, judging by the way they were putting forth, had never been in such fine form.

Toby was looking back at us now with an expression that said, perhaps he had made a slight miscalculation, but what the heck? Was that really any excuse for all this furor?

Jim clutching his school books and lunch pail, his long scarf flying out behind, was racing towards us like a Don Quixote jousting windmills. Suddenly the picture of how we must look to the oncoming teamster hit me and I doubled up with hopeless laughter.

The more Mom hissed, " Mary! For goodness' sakes, stop that silly laughing! Help me up. Get this stupid dog off me. Quick, before that man gets here," the funnier it seemed and so the harder I laughed. And that was the catalyst to inspire Eileen to howl even louder. Her screams now would have scared jackrabbits out of hiding.

Eileen's bellows spurred Tidge into redoubling his efforts, his mangy tail thumping in perfect time with the long stabbing strokes of his tongue.

Fortunately for Mom's sense of decorum, Jimmy arrived ahead of the teamster. My brother lost no time in kicking Tidge out of the way, pulling off Eileen and helping Mom to her feet. Then the cutter was righted, the robes thrown back in, and Eileen shushed big-brother fashion. "For Pete's sake, Kid, shut up! You're scaring the earth-worms in China."

Mom unceremoniously hurried me into the cutter. Her normally gentle grey-green eyes were giving a sudden chill to the afternoon. "I must say, Mary, you were certainly no help. I can't think what you found so amusing."

I was saved the necessity of thinking up a suitable reply (which was just as well judging from the set of Mom's jaw) by the teamster who had pulled up behind us.

"Having a spot of trouble, Ma'am? Need any help?"

Mom's over-the-shoulder glance at the teamster showed a face as cracked as old harness leather, creasing into an amused grin, but he touched his hat in a gentlemanly manner.

Her reply bristled with frosted reserve. "No, thank you. We can manage." Whereupon she snatched up the whip and lambasted Toby a crack that sent him scuttling down the road at a speed quite foreign to his nature.

For the rest of the drive home I kept my mouth burrowed deep under my scarf. It seemed best if Mom didn't hear the stifled giggles that persisted with the regularity of bubbles exploding in a porridge pot.

Mom was still scowling at supper-time when she told Dad how mortified she had been that a complete stranger should have seen her in such an undignified predicament. And how I had laughed as if I thought it was all a great big joke. Dad didn't crack a smile, but the sly wink he tossed in my direction hinted that perhaps we were kindred spirits. At least in some things.

We kids never knew if Tidge's unasked-for help that day had any connection with his rather hush-hush disappearance a short time later. When we asked about it Mom's reply was vague and uncharacteristically terse. "Tidge was getting old so we thought it would be nice to get a pup in the spring. One you children can play with." It was good enough for us.

Mom never again made the mistake of allowing Toby to turn the cutter too short, but once he almost upset the buggy. That time I wasn't laughing. I was too scared to laugh.

We were cresting a sharp hill on our way back from town when Toby suddenly flew back into his breeching, cramping the wheels so violently it seemed the vehicle must surely upset. His eyes, like huge frozen moons, were white-ringed in terror; his flaring nostrils took on a red transparency as he kept backing, fighting to turn and run.

He had reason to be scared.

Something that looked like a black furled umbrella seemed to hang suspended in air just over the brow of the hill. Mom might have got Toby past that if it hadn't been for the "things" arcing through the sky above it like a warren of rabbits chasing themselves across the dome of Heaven. The "things" were Toby's undoing.

He backed, and kept backing, tying himself into frightened knots, almost putting the buggy over a sharp drop into a slough brimming with spring melt. Finally Mom got him out onto a piece of prairie where there was room to turn him so he wouldn't be facing the "things" frightening him.

"Mary, help Eileen down. Quickly! I want you both out of the buggy in case Toby starts acting up again." While Mom was wondering what to do, a man came over the hill. It was a neighbour, Axel Erickson, full of apologies for scaring our horse. When his load of oat bundles had upset he had hung his coat on the center pole of the hayrack while reloading them, not realizing how scary the coat and the flying bundles would look to our pony. Or to any horse coming that way.

Now that bundles were no longer flying across Toby's line of vision, and with Axel at his halter, our pony went past the wagon and rack with no more trouble

It wasn't until Toby was clip-clopping down the trail again that I looked at Mom with approval "That was scary, Mom, but you did real good. I bet you could drive broncos."

"Thank you, Mary. But I have no wish to drive broncos." Mom's voice sounded prim and businesslike but there was the hint of a smile lurking around her mouth as she added, "Toby can be quite enough bronco for me."

It was the Christmas holidays. Toby had been turned out to spend it with the range horses pasturing on 27, a section of open land just east of us. It provided good winter pasture for horses that farmers in the area wouldn't be needing for a few weeks, or a few months. So no one expected trouble the day Axel Erickson drove into our yard. He often stopped on his way to town to see if we needed anything, or had letters to mail. This time he brought bad news.

"There's a bay horse out on 27 with a broken leg. I'm almost certain it's your school pony."

Dad looked grim as he reached for the gun.

"Mom," I wailed, "when Mrs. Erickson broke HER leg the doctor fixed it. Why can't he fix Toby's leg?"

Mom's efforts to explain that horses weren't people did nothing to raise my spirits. I seemed to be facing a lifetime of grey, horseless days.

Dad came back wearing a strained look around his mouth. "Sure hated to have to do that. Toby was a good pony. It won't be easy getting one to replace him."

Replace him? A new horse? Wow! My spirits leaped like sap in a sun-warmed maple. Fickle as a spring breeze, I shoved thoughts of Toby out of my mind to make room for visions of a new and more exciting animal.

Toby hadn't been perfect. He had fallen from my "favourite horse" pedestal. Yet he deserved more tears than I shed for him.

Chapter Four

Jack, Horse of Many Surprises

Jack replaced Toby. Outwardly he looked like hundreds of other school ponies. Quiet, staid, reliable—a horse totally devoid of quirks. We should have suspected that wasn't quite so the Saturday we went to bring him home.

Dad had seen the pony and bought him from Joe Martineau, the livery barn owner, earlier in the week. On Saturday Jim and Mom, with Eileen and me in tow, went with Ray and Rowdy, Dad's reliable team of greys, to bring him home from from the livery barn near Grannie and Grandpa Stubbs' house, where he was being kept for us.

The moment the sleigh stopped at Grannie and Grandpa's house I wanted to race off to the livery barn to see our new pony. But Mom put a quick stop to that. Her prim "Certainly not. Jimmy will get him." told me this was no time to argue. In her eyes livery barns were murky haunts of vice and iniquity. They were no place for ladies and definitely not for her young daughter. "Jimmy will fetch the pony, then you can go out and see him."

Mom ignored my muttered protest: "Darn it. Why do boys get to have all the fun?"

I kept my nose impatiently flattened against Grandma's windowpane for what seemed like forever before Jim hove in sight with a bay pony lagging behind. "His name is Jack," Jim told me with an important smile as I rushed out.

"Why would anyone give a horse a dumb name like that? Maybe we could change it to something more exciting ... like Sultan's Crown, or Apache Chief?" Jack looked as dull as his name. But Mom thought it best to keep the name the pony was familiar with. Well, whatever his name, Jack certainly wasn't a Black Beauty, or a Wildfire.

I climbed resentfully into the sleigh, shooting sour looks at the pony. Maybe we ought to sneak him back. Switch him for a better one. Joe Martineau had so many horses, he probably wouldn't notice.

Mom ignored my vinegar looks, clucked to the greys, and we started off. All except Jack. He braced his feet, threw himself backwards, broke his halter, and trotted happily back to the livery barn.

"By Gosh! He won't break this one." Jim was already removing the new rawhide halter off Rowdy as he spoke.

In minutes Jack was back and re-tied to the sleigh, looking as if nothing short of a blast of dynamite could inspire any form of exertion.

"Something must have scared him," Mom said. "This time everyone sit very still and don't say anything. I'll start up slowly, so he gets the idea we're moving and he's supposed to come with us."

When the greys inched ahead and Jack felt the slack leave his halter rope he reared back, his feet scrabbling for purchase, his arcing body twisting, weaving, straining. Grunts exploded from his flaring nostrils like firecrackers bursting in a starless sky. Finally he flipped, did a backwards summersault, scrambled to his feet and headed for the livery stable again. What was left of the halter trailed behind the sleigh.

"Well, that does it! Your father can get that pony himself." Mom's voice was frosty as cracked ice. "James (she always called my brother James when she was upset), you go and tell that Martineau man I don't think much of his quiet pony. A child's pony indeed." Her mouth twitched in indignation.

In less time than it takes a threshing crew to eat a lemon pie Martineau showed up, his loping strides purposeful, with Jim trotting behind like an anxious puppy.

Well before Joe reached the sleigh where Mom was looking as if her sense of tolerance had deserted her, he touched his cap and smiled a smile designed to thaw a Labrador iceberg. "Sorry about the broken halters, Ma'am. But don't worry. Tell Harold I'll make it right with him. And I'll have my man bring the pony up tomorrow."

True to Joe's word, Jack showed up Sunday afternoon. "No trouble at all," the men told us. We hadn't expected to see two of them. It also seemed a bit unusual to see a heavy logging chain around an animal's neck, with its other end fastened to a sleigh powered by two huge dray horses. Unless that animal happened to be an elephant. Jack at 850 pounds was no elephant. But he was sweated up ... so were the dray team ... unusually so for such a cold winter's day....

However, when Dad handed me the halter-shank, Jack allowed me to lead him to the barn like any well-mannered pony.

Despite a bad beginning Jack did seem to be the reliable kids' pony Joe had claimed him to be. He didn't buck. Not even when I galloped him down hills. Nor did he throw up his head and jerk away from my small hand on his halter—another of Toby's tricks.

So we started driving him to school.

The first week or two all went well. Then a queer trait surfaced in our pony.

When being hitched to the cutter for the morning trip to school Jack stood still as a Trojan horse until all the snaps, buckles, and traces were properly in place. Even then he would wait, his head hanging at half-mast, while we went in to pick up our lunch pails and the hot rock and say goodbye to Mom.

After the cutter robes were firmly tucked around us Jim would pick up the reins and flap them against Jack's well-padded rump, and the pony would get into the ambling trot that was his normal gait for the four-and-a-half-mile trip to school. No pony could be expected to behave better than that.

At that time school horses were still stabled in the livery barn's lean-to. Jack knew the place well, because before Dad bought him the livery barn had been his home. The proprietor's son, Toady Martineau, had often ridden Jack during the buffalo roundups at Wainwright Buffalo Park.

So what was there about the livery barn to turn a sensible morning pony into an afternoon screwball?

When backed into the shafts at the livery barn in the afternoon, Jack would have his head in the air, his eyes wilder than a caged moose.

It was my job to stand at his head to hold him from moving until Jim had the tugs fastened, the breeching snaps done up and was in the conveyance with the reins. Then, if luck was with me ... and it often wasn't ... I had time to run back and get in before Jack lunged ahead. If I didn't, we were in big trouble.

If Jack was made to stop and wait for me to get in, even if it was only for a split-second, he'd fidget and dance, looking belligerent and ready for some sort of retaliation. The words "get-up" now would send him flying into reverse as if red hot pokers were threatening his nose ... just as he had done the day he broke the halters.

Slapping him with the lines, or the whip, only made him back that much faster. Sometimes one of the older boys, thinking to help, would make a grab for Jack's halter to try to lead him forward.

Jack would rear, shy away, and keep right on backing. But if the boy was strong enough to hang on, Jack burst upward like an exploding land mine, his front feet flailing air until the boy was shaken off. Then he'd come down running, often throwing in a few bucks, kicks, and crow-hops just for the hell of it.

Enthusiasm for helping us soon faded.

The days I was quick enough to run back and climb in before Jack started up we were okay. Then after a half-hearted lunge or two he would quickly settle into his normal gait. It became important to get in any way I could, just so long as Jack didn't have to stop for me.

Consequently I was constantly poised on the edge of challenge, my body tense and electric as I left his head and raced back to grab the cutter. It's amazing how adept a youngster can get at grabbing a cutter and hauling herself into it as it swirls past.

The buggy was different. It was too high for me to get a hand-hold on the back. Impossible to climb into when the wheels were moving. I lived in terror that either I'd get caught between the wheels while trying to get in, or Jack would cramp the wheels when I was in and upset the buggy.

Watching the Kennedy outfit start away from the livery barn became the highlight of the day for country and town kids alike. The 3:30 bell triggered a stampede for the livery barn—everyone wanted to watch the fun. Although I had dreamed of a horse that would make folks turn for a second look, this sort of notoriety wasn't at all what I had in mind. If this was God's way of punishing me for ostentation He was certainly overdoing it.

Our parents had trouble believing the stories we told them about Jack. He was the model of good behaviour at home. But Joe Martineau knew. He had witnessed Jack's shenanigans, so whenever he or one of his men were around they helped us get Jack into forward gear.

As soon as we were away from the livery barn we could stop Jack outside a store or post office and he would re-start like any normal horse.

Finally it was the end of June.

Before school re-opened in September the school barn was finished. Jack was no longer housed in the livery stable. Only rarely now did we have any explosive backing experiences.

If there was a plausible explanation for the effect that livery barn had on Jack, I never heard it.

I wasn't often lucky enough to have both Jim and Eileen sick at the same time. I say "lucky" because it was only then that I got to ride rather than drive to school. I'll never forget the first time it happened.

Entering town I felt like a queen on her royal palfry. I imagined, and indeed hoped, there would be eyes at every window to pay me homage. I had forgotten the old adage "pride goes before a fall."

Instead of Jack breaking into the lively trot I was asking for, he shied, when there was nothing at all to shy at. I hit the ground. Hard.

The hurt to my bones was nothing compared to the hurt to my pride. To be dumped off in the middle of town was absolutely the worst thing that could possibly have happened to me.

Mortified, totally devastated, I scrambled to my feet, then looked furtively around hoping no one had witnessed my downfall (moments before I had been hoping the entire town was watching my grand entry). Then, to make matters even worse, I realized that without the convenience of a saddle I couldn't climb back on. At home I used a wagon wheel, a corral fence, or a stone. Here there was nothing.

Ignominiously I slunk off towards the school barn, leading Jack and dragging my pride in the dust.

Usually Jack's feet were too firmly planted on the ground for any unnecessary bursts of speed. A feature my parents thought admirable, but which I longed to rectify.

"Dad, when you're dynamiting rocks today can I come with you on Jack and watch?"

"Certainly not. Jack would get scared."

"Aw, Dad. He wouldn't. Not if I stayed beside your team."

Secretly I was hoping the pony would get scared. I wanted to find out what it would be like riding him when he wasn't acting like a travel-tired turtle. But I wasn't about to tell that to Dad.

Perhaps Dad was secretly a bit proud of his tomboy daughter, for he said, "If you come you'll have to stay well back and keep Jack facing away from the blasting." Neither of us told Mom.

With the fuse lit, Dad hurried back to his team and grabbed the lines. My legs gripped Jack's barrel sides in anticipation of the big bang. When it came, the greys jumped. Jack ran a couple of yards.

"By George! That's a sensible pony." There was admiration in Dad's voice as he stepped over to pat Jack when I swung in beside the team again.

Who needed that much sense? Next time I'd swing Jack around so he could see the ground in front of him explode and mushroom heavenward. Maybe that would scare him into doing something worthwhile.

It did.

As the dense black pyramid of earth and debris rocketed skyward Jack whirled; he was streaking for the horizon almost before the muffled boom caught up with us. I had to make a wild grab for his mane to keep from falling off. I knew now he *could* move. So for the time being I was satisfied.

There would be other occasions, too, when Jack showed what he could do if he wanted to.

A competition grew among the country boys to see who could hitch up their horse and get down the hill and out the school gate first. Ben-Hur chariot races would have paled by comparison. The gate had been designed to accommodate one vehicle, not the two, sometimes three or even four, racing for it now at a dead heat. It's a miracle there were no horrific smash-ups. It certainly wasn't because of good sense. Or school supervision.

Jack was one of the smaller school ponies. In my eyes he wasn't much for looks. But it became a point of honour with him (and with Jim, his driver) to be first out the school gate and first downtown. The town boys vied for a chance to ride the runners of the Kennedy cutter and cheer Jack on.

James Chartres, son of the local lawyer, and Lester Key, son of the grain buyer for the Searle Grain Company, agreed to take turns riding the runner of our cutter. The other would settle for the Wilbur Clark outfit pulled by Old Baldy, a blue roan showing a smattering of thoroughbred blood.

One day Old Baldy had the lead and was first out the gate. Lester, clinging to the near runner of that cutter, whooped with glee as he slung good-natured insults back at Chartres. When Chartres thumped our cutter-box screaming "Ya! Ya! Run ya little bastard, run!" Jack sprouted wings. As the Kennedy cutter drew abreast of the Clark outfit, Chartres' foot shot out. He had intended to plant a friendly kick on Lester's rear-end but somehow his boot got caught in the pocket of Lester Key's pants. Both boys clung to their respective sleighs with all the tenacity of English bull-dogs, neither one willing to face the ignominy of being the one pulled off and dragged. Their arcing bodies formed a living bridge between the two cutters. Neither driver would give an inch. It looked like a set-up for disaster.

Finally Jack inched ahead. As he did there was a horrific ripping sound and Chartres' boot swung clear. It had the seat of Key's trousers floating from it like a flag of victory.

There were shrieks of dismay from the Clark cutter. Key's face was the colour of boiled lobster as he flung himself onto the seat to hide his bare bottom. But it was too late. A bevy of high school girls had witnessed the whole episode. Hoots of derision followed him as the cutters careered towards Main Street, where Key leaped out and raced for Pop Coutts' General Store with both hands plastered over his exposed rear end.

Within minutes he re-emerged, decently clothed, but it was weeks before he lived down that episode. Not surprisingly, interest in cutter racing dwindled.

Although Jack had been the horse to beat when leaving the school yard ... and usually no other horse did... out on the road he didn't care how many outfits passed him.

Then came the day a flashy team of drivers, resplendent in sleigh bells and fancy harness, came dashing up behind us. Jim pulled Jack over to let them pass, but our pony had other ideas. He laid his ears flat back in challenge and broke into a gallop that would have become a full-blown race if Jim hadn't stopped him.

"What did you have to do that for?" I demanded. "Maybe Jack could've beaten them."

"Na. Not a hope. Those were standard-breds with legs as long as telephone poles. Anyway there's too much snow for racing."

Maybe my brother was right. Maybe Jack couldn't have shown those drivers his heels, but he was a horse of many surprises.

I got one the day Phyllis, a town a girl in my class who had everything, and made the most of it, rode out to meet me on a horse called Ranger, a high-stepping animal she had borrowed from the livery stable. Alongside her horse Jack looked almost as uninspiring as a dead toad. Phyllis and I were on our way to visit Iona, a friend who lived a few miles farther on; then the three of us were going to go riding.

When Ranger broke into a brisk gallop Jack plunked along behind, not caring one iota that he was wallowing in another animal's dust. I was too mortified to admit we might have been trying to race.

In time we arrived at Iona's home. Her horse was the sleek thoroughbred type, so I hoped no one would suggest a race. I tried to keep a low profile, knowing Jack was hopelessly outclassed.

We were riding towards home when Phyllis looked at Jack as one might look at a warty toad and said, "I don't suppose *you'd* want to race, Mary. Why don't you just watch Iona and me?"

While I was groping for some reasonable response she kicked her horse into a gallop and was off, with the thoroughbred close on her heels.

Perhaps Jack had simply had enough of Phyllis's superior airs, or perhaps the fact that he was heading towards home had something to do with it. Whatever the reason, he sprang to life and streaked after the other two horses. To my surprise and unbounded delight he passed them both. I had never been so proud of him.

From then on, if someone suggested a race, I didn't hesitate. Jack would take off like a thoroughbred shot from the starting gate. Or maybe he imagined he was back chasing buffalo, reliving the days he had been part of the great fall roundups at Wainwright Buffalo Park.

Running those great brutes had developed Jack's hindquarters so that on an uphill race he was almost never beaten. When handling animals as dangerous and unpredictable as buffalo, critters capable of incredible bursts of speed on uphill runs (but inclined to be awkward when going downhill), this quality could mean the difference between death and survival.

One summer I tried to make Jack into a jumper by aiming him at a clump of rose bushes, whacking him into a rollicking gallop, and expecting him to clear said rose bushes. He never did.

Jack saw no reason to jump anything if going around it cost less effort. So my attempts to get him to jump weren't a big success. But I did get better at sticking on a swerving, barebacked horse. And that was an accomplishment in itself.

Apart from the town episode, Jack rarely dumped me off. But one day he did ... I think. I had intended to play "cowboy" and herd a pretend string of ornery steers. To do this Jack was going to have to move fast and turn quickly. Two things he didn't normally view with a whole lot of favour.

I often rode him in from the pasture with just a halter rope. But today, needing more control, I made awrap around his nose with the rope, and then with a willow switch in my hand I led him up to a mounting stone. And climbed on.... or did I?

The first thing I remember after standing on the stone alongside Jack was picking myself up off the ground some distance from the rock, with the uneasy feeling I might have been there for quite some time. Jack was several yards away, quietly grazing.

To this day the interval between standing on that rock and coming to on the ground is a complete blank. Had the rope been too tight and he threw up his head and hit mine hard enough to knock me out? Or had he bucked? Or had I blacked out for some quite different reason? I had no idea. It seemed wiser not to mention it to my parents.

We knew winter mornings were cold when smoke from every chimney rose straight up to stab the sky like burnished rapiers before hurrying to join the haze of frost crystals hanging high under a pale, anemic sun. When the air snapped and crackled with cold we would tie the reins to the cutter-post, pull a patchwork quilt over our heads, snuggle down under the buffalo robe with our feet on the hot rock, our hands doubled into fists inside two pairs of mittens, and be confident Jack would get us to school. On the rare mornings we met an oncoming sleigh he would stop and wait for us to re-surface and steer him off the trail.

Sometimes blizzards left chest-high drifts. Living as we did on an isolated road there was always a mile and a half of trail to break. Sometimes we broke trail for the full four and a half miles.

When drifts were too hard and too deep for Jack to get through with the cutter we had to unhitch and drive him lunging and scrambling ahead of us until he had made a sort of trail. He never panicked in snow, as some horses do. Nor did I ever know him to give up and lie down.

One morning a chinook was glazing the snow, bringing thoughts of spring to the chickadees. Jim and I were sick, so Eileen, in grade two now, rode to school. As can so easily happen with Alberta weather, by home-time a blizzard was screeching across the land, scuttling drifting snow before it.

Eileen, not wanting to face the biting lash of wind and snow, turned and sat huddled backwards on Jack, leaving him to plod into the storm unguided. Jack, head down and half-turned against the sting of ice pellets, got his small charge home safely. Apart from being so cold Dad had to half carry her into the house, Eileen was none the worse for that experience.

Being top-rung on the horse hierarchy held little charm for Jack. Not if it meant an expenditure of energy. He would willingly give ground to any horse who gave him a sour look. If that horse happened to be Peterson's Old Bill, a standard-bred who could trot eighteen miles an hour and had an explosive disposition that made him more aggressive than a musk-ox bull in rut, Jack would actually cringe.

All the school horses stood in fear of old Bill. He had a mean eye, vicious teeth, and deadly heels. No one disputed his right to a stall of his own. The other horses had their own stalls too, the only difference being old Bill *needed* his.

The barn was a popular hang-out for the boys at noon and recess. One day a couple of them decided to see what would happen if they put Old Bill, the meanest horse on the premises, in with Jack, the most timid. "Heck Wilbur, we'll take Old Bill out before he gets to hurting the little guy real bad." But they hadn't counted on the school bell marshalling them back to classes quite so soon.

Back in their seats they fidgeted, they scratched, they looked at the clock, they shot anxious glances at each other. If only the teacher hadn't been so adamant about the rule, "No leaving the room for the first half-hour."

Finally Albert couldn't stand the suspense. Waving his hand like a shipwrecked sailor sighting a sail, he called out, "Please, Sir. May I leave the room? Honest, I've gotta go real bad. I must've et a poisonous mushroom." Indeed, he did seem to be turning the colour of a dead fish, so the teacher thought it sagacious to bend his rule.

No sooner had Albert raced from the room than Wilbur leapt to his feet. "I've gotta go too, Sir. I must've et the same mushroom."

Had the teacher troubled to look he would have wondered why the boys should be streaking past the outhouses towards the barn as if buckshot was threatening their rear-ends.

"Great Jumpin' Bull Frogs! Would'ya believe that!?" Albert brushed a hand across his eyes, still not quite believing what he was seeing.

Old Bill was down, lying on his back, his feet in the air like a cowed puppy. Jack, standing half over him, wore a deceptively innocent expression. What Jack did, or how he did it, no one knows. But from that time forward Old Bill never laid his ears back at Jack.

Jack would never have won a beauty contest; he was rarely easy to catch, he continued to break halters rather than lead behind a vehicle, and he was prone to other behavioural quirks. Yet he challenged us, he taught us, and he always got us safely home. He gave honour to the epithet "School Pony."

Mary Kennedy on Jack. In 1927, girls never wore jeans of any kind. Horses always wore nose-bage in the summer to protect them from troublesome nose-flies. In the background is the house where Mary was born.

Chapter Five

An Attractive Little Devil on Horseback

Our house sparkled with excitement. It shone with polish. The youngest Colonel ever to retire from the Indian Medical Service was about to visit our farm at Hughenden. Dad's oldest brother Bob had recently accepted the position as doctor on a millionaire's yatcht on an around-the-world cruise. And when that cruise hit Canada's west coast he would be coming to visit us.

Mom scrubbed and dusted. If cleaning could transform a homesteader's three-rooms-plus-porch home into a palace, ours would have been a palace. Sometimes Mom allowed herself a sigh ... then she would banish thoughts of Brackenfell, her parents' stately English home before a stock market crash had altered their lives and the lives of their children.

Mom's pioneer home had few amenities, but it had love, trust, warmth, and understanding. Sometimes even a bit of culture. Dad said, "You don't need to worry about Bob. He's used to roughing it. Both in India and in Tibet."

Uncle Bob was everything a horse-crazy nine-year-old could hope for in an uncle. He wore jodhpurs. And riding boots that mirrored the sun. He played polo and he knew *lots* about horses. If only he would have gone riding with me, my world would have been perfect.

Mom gently explained that our farm animals weren't the type of horses army officers rode. To my indignant "Not even Darky?" Mom hedged, "Well, perhaps he doesn't want to take the time. He and your father have a lot of talking to catch up on."

Yet Uncle Bob didn't seem to mind if I sat on his knee, even though riding Jack bareback had left my legs and bloomers crusted in horse sweat. When Mom scolded, "Mary, go get washed and change your clothes. You'll make Uncle Bob dirty," he just smiled.

"Don't worry, Muriel. She's all right." (In 1927 wearing pants was the sole prerogative of the male sex. A girl wearing trousers in public would immediately be labelled "fast.")

Uncle Bob told exciting stories about his visit to the Dalai Lama in the "forbidden" city of Lhasa, a sacred place high in the Himalaya mountains of Tibet.

He and his friend Sir Charles Bell were the fourth white men to reach the city. Getting there had not been easy. At times their lives had been in danger. But what interested me most was hearing about the Shetland ponies that had been among the many gifts they took to the Dalai Lama. Gifts designed to soften that great ruler's heart so he would grant permission for a 1924 National Geographic Society expedition to climb Everest, Tibet's Holy Mountain.

The Dalai Lama must have liked the Shetlands. The Expedition got the permission they needed. It didn't interest me that another uncle, who was a medical doctor as well as a high-ranking army officer, naturalist and author, should have been one of those chosen to go on the actual expedition to climb Everest in 1924, a mountain the Tibetan people revered as a holy place.

I wanted to hear more about the Shetland ponies. Owning one had been a long-time dream of mine. That was before I rode a friend's Shetland bareback and discovered how hard it is to stay on the back of a round-as-a-barrel little animal with no withers and a propensity to drop its head.

I also liked hearing about Uncle Bob's little dog. A dog that had saved his life and the lives of others on the expedition by taking a poisoned spear intended for his master, and thereby alerting the troops marching towards Tibet that there were warlike tribesmen lurking in the tall jungle grass.

Before Uncle Bob returned to the yacht he took Jimmy and me into the Hughenden drug store and told us to pick out anything we wanted. Jim gained immediate approval by selecting a fine Waterman fountain pen. Uncle Bob wasn't so pleased with my choice. He kept steering me away from the toy horse to look at other things. Wouldn't I like this? Or that? There were so many things he thought more suitable for a girl. But always I gravitated back to the dappled pony and cart. Finally, with a resigned sigh and looking as if he would never fully understand the female of the species, he bought me the toy. And I was happy.

After he had returned to Ireland and his mother asked him, "And what sort of a child is Harold's daughter Mary?" his response was "She's an attractive little devil on horseback."

Poor Mom. She had tried to mould her horse-mad offspring into a ladylike child. Whatever would her mother-in-law think? A lady who entertained the Earl of Bantry's wife at her "at-home teas" as well as the wives of other elite gentry and professional men in the Bantry area. On the other hand, Dad seemed rather pleased with the epithet.

In reality I expect I was a horrible little brat. Nick, the hired man who came to work for Dad soon after Uncle Bob had left, would have thought so.

Nick had been hired to drive Dad's four-horse team on the breaking plough while Dad walked the furrows digging out newly exposed rocks with his crowbar before they could be recovered by the next furrow.

Nick, from the Ukraine, was probably a good teamster. Throwing small stones to speed up the slow horse on the outfit may have been an excellent idea—it wouldn't startle the other horses as slapping the laggard with a line might have done. But throwing stones at horses was totally foreign to my sister Eileen and me. It seemed so utterly barbaric we decided we had to do something about it.

That something was to walk behind the plough and each time Nick threw a stone at a horse we threw two at him. Some of our stones must have hit their mark, because Nick turned to glare at us several times, but we were always down on our knees with our backs to him, innocently exclaiming at the way little red ants were racing around trying to re-hide their eggs.

It was fun while it lasted. But it ended suddenly when Dad found out what we were doing.

June 1927. Harold Kennedy cultivating with Ray, Rowdy, Darky and Beauty on the cultivator. Mary watches from Jack.

"Come on. I'll show you our horses."

Mary Lawley, a town girl two years my senior gave me a sour look that suggested looking at horses was only slightly worse than scrubbing floors, but if that was all there was to do then she'd better make the best of it.

A few minutes later we were standing on the bottom rail of the corral fence, our arms and upper torsos leaning against the top rail. "There's Darky. He's the black, and he's mine. Beauty is the bay Clydesdale, the two greys are Ray and Rowdy, and there's Jack, but you know him. We drive him to school." I felt like a king showing off my crown jewels to a visiting monarch—a monarch who seemed totally bored and quite indifferent to my treasures. Then Mary jerked to attention so suddenly I almost lost my balance and fell off the fence.

"What's that long snaky thing hanging down under Darky's belly" she demanded, her voice sharp, her eyes scrutinizing.

I looked and felt my face grow hot. "Oh, that's just what geldings use when they have to do Number One." In our house bodily eliminations were referred to as Number One and Number Two. Although I had heard the words "piss" and "shit" in school and now knew what they meant, along with some of the other "dirty" four-letter words which I didn't, I never used them. I was sure if I did my parents, especially my mother, wouldn't know what I was talking about.

"But what's it *really* for?" Mary Lawley was leaning towards me now the way a dog that has just sniffed an interesting scent strains at its leash. Perhaps she had heard the word "penis," perhaps she had even heard snide whispers about its function. I hadn't. So I just shrugged, "Nothing else that I know of." And for me the matter was closed. The strange look the older girl shot me was a mixture of amazement and pity.

Chapter Six

Rowdy and Roping Gophers

Mom said my addiction to horses was giving her grey hair. It had started when I was a toddler.

Dad had put Ray and Rowdy in the barn and gone in for dinner without bothering to shut the barn door. There seemed no reason why it should be shut. It was a hot day; the horses would be cooler with it open.

He was towelling his face with the red and yellow striped terry towel that hung near the wash bench when Mom looked up from mashing potatoes. "Have you seen Mary?"

Dad started to say, "She was playing just outside when ... " but he didn't finish. Instead he tore out the door, his mind leaping with apprehension. His face, leathered by long exposure to wind and sun, took on a sickly pallor as his eyes swept the yard for a child no longer in it. Dear God! He raced for the barn on long-striding feet.

At the barn door he froze, fear freezing his brain. I was standing under Rowdy's belly, a gelding with such low fly tolerance he'd kick at the merest suspicion an insect might be zoning in on the tender under-parts of his back legs.

Dad, fighting to keep raw panic from his voice, called softly, "Mary. Come to Daddy," while easing himself closer to the greys. It was vital he not startle them—a kick, any movement .... "Whoa Rowdy. Steady, Ray."

Dad watched a small hand reach up to pat the sensitive underside of Rowdy's back leg. Steel bands of fear choked his breathing. It was the sort of dilemma that should only happen to a man in a nightmare. But this

53

was no nightmare. Emotion shouted, "Rush in! Grab her! Get her out of there!" Reason countered, "Startle the greys now and they'll trample her."

It took a supreme effort of will to force himself to do nothing at all except to talk quietly to his team. But he lived a lifetime of suspense until I toddled happily out from under Rowdy's belly, bestowing one final pat on the gelding's powerful back leg before rushing into my father's arms. Dad buried his face in my blond curls. From now on the barn door would be kept shut.

Rowdy was the lazy horse in Dad's outfit. He was so laid-back he rarely saw the need of doing anything in a hurry. It was no sweat under his collar if his mates sometimes pulled more than their share. When Dad drove him single in buggy or cutter, which wasn't often, he saw it as his duty to stop at every crossroad, look both directions, and then let fly a high gravelly whinny that scared gophers into their holes, or snowbirds into hiding. We kids would giggle. "He thinks he's a train that has to whistle for the crossings."

Dad said, "He's calling for Ray. They've been inseparable ever since I bought them as three-year-olds." And indeed the grey geldings were such good friends we frequently saw them playing together in the pasture as if they were wild stallions fighting for the right to be the leader of their band of mares, yet they never fought "for real." I have never known another pair of geldings to play-act the vigorous way Dad's greys did.

Rowdy had a built-in time-clock. He always knew exactly when it was time to be unhitched for dinner, or supper. And he'd tell Dad so by slowing down and whinnying when he got to the end of the field nearest the barn. His clock never got out of whack.

Dad said Rowdy was honest and steady. A good reliable horse. But to my ten-year-old eyes those attributes didn't add much to his qualifications. He was low horse on my popularity pole.

"Dad, Eileen is big enough to ride Jack now; why can't I ride Darky?"

My father finished stropping his razor-blade before speaking. "Because Darky's too much horse for you. You'll have to wait until you're older, Mavourneen." Having said that Dad tamped tobacco into his pipe, flicked a match on his thumbnail and ignited the tobacco, thoughtfully sucking on the pipe until it was drawing to his satisfaction. After putting the lid back on the can of Old Chum pipe tobacco, he smiled in a placating fashion and offered what he obviously considered a suitable alternative. "When I'm not using Rowdy you can ride him."

"Ride Rowdy? He's a workhorse! And he's lazy! Besides, I've ridden him since I was a baby." Or so it seemed in my ten-year-old eyes because back then if I had pestered Dad for rides when he was cleaning barns and hauling the manure to spread on the fields it was Rowdy's back I got tossed onto. To keep from falling off the broad-backed horse when he trotted I had to grip the back-pad with both hands. Or, after I could reach them, the hames (the curved bars that fit into the grooves on either side of a horse collar and hold the traces). It had been fun then. Now that I was grown-up I wanted something more challenging.

"But Dad! Rowdy is so slow! Even Jack will run away from him." The words sounded like the rasping of broken windmill vanes flailing out the futility of their existence to every passing breeze. My future looked bleak. I faced a lifetime of swallowing another horse's dust. My spirits drooped. My bottom lip inched out. But I told myself with a martyred sigh I'd better try to be thankful. Rowdy had to be slightly better than nothing.

In my eyes the tall-hipped gelding had about as much elegance as a trail-weary Texas longhorn. I saddled him with little enthusiasm, longing for the day when I could ride Darky, not dreaming there might be more to Rowdy than met the eye.

But something about the saddle seemed to trigger a transformation in the grey, as though the plain old work horse suddenly saw himself as a creature of blood and beauty, poised on the edge of nobility. He reached out for challenge now with a whoop and a holler, all traces of laziness forgotten. He had an eager, excited air about him as if life was full of challenges and he was in a rush to take them all on.

I felt like one of King Arthur's knights riding a great white charger, for Rowdy seemed better suited to thundering down the jousting field than manoeuvring like a fast-wheeling cow pony. And a cow pony was really what I wanted. But maybe Rowdy could learn.

The day I suggested to six-year-old Eileen, "let's herd gophers," she beamed as if I'd just come up with a brilliantly innovative idea. But what did it mean? So I tried to explain.

"We can drive them away from their holes, and pretend the gophers are the steers our ranch boss wants us to move to another pasture. It'll be great practice for our horses." Then I was hit by an even more splendid idea. "Maybe we should herd them all back onto the neighbour's land. Daddy says that's where they came from in the first place."

As we stuffed lasso lengths of binder twine into our pockets and saddled the horses, Eileen looked impressed that such words of wisdom could whirl around in her sister's head.

Upon reaching gopher-town we began galloping our horses after the varmints, whooping and yelling in what we believed was proper cowboy style. But each time we charged after a gopher it flicked its tail in a cheeky fashion and whisked down a hole, and it wasn't easy to get our horses hauled to a stop and pulled around. They obviously thought we had been setting them up for a mile-long race and saw no reason to stop before they had properly started.

Eileen Kennedy on Jack, Mary on Rowdy, but neither horse had any idea how to herd gophers.

Rowdy might have done well at jousting—he had the size and strength to carry a fully armoured knight at a full gallop down a jousting field. As a fast-wheeling gopher-horse he was a complete dud. When changing directions it seemed he needed about a half-acre of unencumbered ground to turn in. Nor did he understand that when I aimed him at a gopher he was supposed to chase the thing, keep his eyes on it, swerving, dodging when it did, not gallop blithely on past as if it didn't exist. Nor should he arc his body into the air to miss trampling it should one make the mistake of getting under his feet. Jack was no better. So while there were gophers whistling at us from all their doorways, we had no luck at all herding them.

"Well then," I snorted, sliding off Rowdy and dragging a length of binder-twine out of my pocket, "We'll rope them."

When a gopher poked his head up through my string I jerked the noose tight, and jumped back screeching, "I have him! I have him!" The grey gelding, his eyes the size of a harvest moon, sidled as far away from me as the lines would permit. He obviously didn't feel safe around this yelling creature swinging a gopher around her head as if she was winding up for an Olympic throw.

Finally, gasping for breath, I stopped gyrating. The string sagged. The gopher hit the ground. To my utter amazement it wasn't dead. It was leaping and clawing at the string. And it was coming straight towards me. Great Thundering Guns! Now what did I do?

Boys killed gophers by stomping on their heads. I couldn't do *that*. It was gross. Neither did I dare take the string off and let it go. I'd get bitten. So somehow I had to kill the rodent. But how? Eileen, looking disgustingly superior, didn't have an answer. Then my eyes lit on Rowdy swinging his head to brush a fly off his flank.

Quick as a flash I was in the saddle. The twine firmly wrapped around one hand brought the gopher, still jerking and jumping, into the immediate vicinity of the gelding's back legs. Rowdy promptly catapulted skyward as if blasted from a cannon, and came back down running. It took several fast laps around a field of freshly worked summer fallow, with the gopher ricocheting back and forth between the gelding's powerful hocks, before Rowdy, or I, thought it safe to stop. Eileen on Jack, who had pounded faithfully along behind, stopped too.

To everyone's immense relief the gopher was dead. So dead there wasn't a great deal left to identify it as having once been a gopher. But there was a tail.

"Aren't you going to save the tail?" Eileen's tone implied we ought to have something to show for all our effort.

"No! I am not! If Jimmy wants to collect two cents for that tail he can get it himself."

After that episode I briefly considered taking up jousting. But I knew we'd be in real big trouble if Mom or Dad found out about it. I didn't want to be grounded for life.

Rowdy continued to fill my needs for a horse until Dad decided that now that I had reached the early teens I was old enough to handle Darky. Finally I was allowed to ride the horse that so long ago had raised the spirits of a very sick little girl—when Dad had said I could call him mine. Now, my spirits leaped and danced like the Northern lights in a midnight sky. I saddled Darky, feeling I was perched comfortably on the edge of everything I had ever hoped for.

The black threw up his head and trotted off with all his old spirit—that same indomitable spirit that never allowed another horse-drawn rig to pass him, and once made him take on the challenge of racing a Buick car. But something was lacking. He no longer moved with the easy gait of his youth.

I felt stricken with reality. Darky's joints and muscles had grown stiff from years of hard work. I wouldn't dare race him. Not even against Jack. I was afraid the horse who had been my idol for so many years would fall from his pedestal. I didn't want anyone to witness his disgrace.

I rode Darky ... more out of loyalty to a dream than because I preferred him to Rowdy. If Eileen sometimes wondered out loud why I had suddenly lost interest in racing, I'd reply with condescending scorn. "Darky! Against Jack? You'd call *that* a race?"

It would be some years after Rowdy and Darky that another black horse came into my life.

Chapter Seven

Runaways and Other Odds and Ends

When horse-power was paramount on the prairies runaways were common. Yet when Mom spoke of the ones Dad had, the fine patrician lines of her brows pulled together in a rare frown of disapproval, as if somehow he ought to have prevented them.

Dad was on the ground shutting the gate. He had been hauling hay from MacGregor's with Ray and Rowdy on the sleigh. They were such a reliable team that when opening a gate he would often stand to one side, tell them to step through it, then shut the gate behind them. Only this time they didn't stop when he called "whoa." When they got to the incline leading to our house the heavily loaded sleigh started to run up on them, and that made them break into a trot which quickly became a gallop. By the time they got to the bottom of the hill they were going full blast.

Mom, seeing the team and hayrack racing driverless down the hill, felt her face blanche. The past seemed to be closing in on her, strangling her in a blanket of smothering memories. In a daze of body-numbing horror her mind went crashing back to the time she had witnessed another runaway down that same hill with Ray and Rowdy on that same hayrack. Then it hadn't exactly been a runaway. Yet its memory would be forever emblazoned in blood-red letters on the minds of two people as one of those near-tragedies in life that miraculously didn't happen and so is best put into the file-holder of memory under *"Thank You, God!"*

Now the kitchen window held Mom's eyes the way a magnet holds a new pin. In a hypnotic daze she watched the team swing into a perfect turn, take their load through the narrow gateway leading up to the house at a dead gallop, then continue on towards the barnyard. Ray and Rowdy couldn't have made the turn for the gate any better had a Ben-Hur been guiding them, yet at the speed they were going even he wouldn't have been able to stop them when they reached the barn. Obviously the runaways had no intention of stopping. Not yet. They galloped merrily on past the barn as if for them the race was still a piece of unfinished business.

Mom's hand flew to her throat as she saw the team head towards an opening between an oat-bin and a buggy-shed that was scarcely wide enough for the hayrack to squeak through when the horses were walking. Now Dad's driverless team took their heavily loaded rack through it at a full-blown gallop, then made three complete circles around a poplar bluff where they were accustomed to taking feed to the cattle, before coming back through the opening between oat-bin and buggy-shed again. But by then Ray and Rowdy were gearing down and ready to stop when they got to the barn. No hay had been spilled. Nothing was damaged. It seemed incredible.

Jim was a toddler, and the apple of his father's eye, the day Dad took him for a sleigh ride that came within an eye-blink of ending in tragedy. He sat the child down in the centre of the hayrack, the part known as the bunk-box. It was the support that the rack proper sat on. It was also sometimes called the stone-box because when the hayrack wasn't needed the rack could be tipped off and the low-sided plank box was ideal for hauling stones off the field, or barrels of water from a neighbour's bored well.

The floor of the rack itself had cross-beams three feet apart that were covered with boards except where the stone-box became the sunken floor. Kennedy thought a child sitting in that box would be perfectly safe; there seemed no way anything could fall out of it.

So Dad, intending to give his son a thrilling ride, let Ray and Rowdy gallop as they came down the hill to the house. Maybe the horses were going faster than he realized. Or maybe he was watching Jim, who was laughing and waving his arms in obvious excitement, instead of paying attention to his driving....

Whatever the reason, the horses swung a mite too wide as they made the turn to go through the gate, and one corner of the hayrack hit a heavy gate-post with enough momentum to throw the rack up into the air, taking Dad with it. He was able to hang onto the lines and fight the team to a stop, his brain numb with the ghastly certainty that he had just killed his only son.

He was sure there was no way the child could have escaped being killed. When the rack flew off, its cross-beams would almost certainly have slammed into the lad. If they hadn't sent him hurtling through the air they would have decapitated him. In those few seconds Dad died a thousand deaths. Guilt, cold and absolute, had him in its grisly grip. Oh God! Why hadn't he been more careful? How would he tell his wife?

Suddenly sounds usually hard for men to tolerate with a whole lot of equanimity shattered the airways. This time they sounded sweeter than heavenly music to my father's ears. Jimmy was screaming.

When the boy, sitting exactly where he had been before the accident, suddenly realized his Dad and the hayrack were both gone, vanished as if by magic, he began to yell. It had always been his sure-fire way of getting attention, and by golly today it worked even faster than he expected. In no time flat his Dad had him in his arms, cradling and soothing him, whispering almost incoherent words of relief and endearment until the child's frightened screams became hiccups.

Miraculously Jim didn't have a scratch on him, but the memory of that day, the horrors of what might have happened, would be emblazoned on his parents' memory for the rest of their lives.

The day smelled of calamity.

A vicious wind, belligerent and in the mood for trouble, had been whipping up dust-devils all morning, swirling autumn leaves off the trees before their time, driving Russian thistles into fence-lines, then swooping away in search of other things to pick up and carry off, leaving the weeds to hang on the barbed-wire in a way that gave the fences the slovenly appearance of being long forgotten clotheslines draped in rotting gunny sacks. It was a goblin wind that bullied the cattle, drove their tails between their legs, and blew against their hair, lifting it like porcupine quills alerted for trouble

My younger sister Barbe and I were cleaning trash from the garden for Mom, with Pearl and Shorty on the stone-box wagon. We were sometimes conscious of the whirr of the binder above the gale, but only when Dad was working on the near side of the field. Suddenly my head flew up. Above the dull roar of the wind I thought I heard a muffled shout. A second later there was no mistaking what I was hearing. It was the thud of galloping horses intermingled with the frightening clashing and clanging of tortured metal.

I threw the lines to Barbe. "Here! You put the horses away." I was off at a long-reaching run not knowing what to expect. Except there had been a runaway with the binder. My heart was pounding like African tom-toms as more and more grisly thoughts persisted in drumming their way into my brain.

When I rounded a poplar-bush and the field stretched ahead of me relieved breath swooshed from my struggling lungs. Dad was limping down the field. At least he could walk. I had feared he might be dead.

To my yell, "Are you hurt? What happened?" I heard a husky "No." The answer to the rest of the question came later after he had caught his breath and we were both hurrying towards what looked like a wrecked aeroplane.

Dad had been at the back of the binder adjusting the platform-canvas where it went over a roller when the wind got under it and whipped it up in the air. That scared Nellie, and her fright fed the others. "I made a grab for the lines and I got them, but by then the horses were gone. I couldn't stop them. I tripped trying to climb back up onto the binder and got dragged quite a piece through the stubble before I had to let them go."

Horror rose up in my throat. "Dad. You're lucky you weren't tightening a front canvas." My stomach knotted at the thought of what the binder's knife would have done to him. Even the reels and the rollers would have mangled his body.

"Did you see the horses?" There were haggard lines etched in the dust around Dad's eyes as he pushed his hat back from a mahogany forehead to reveal a startlingly white brow beyond the reach of sun and wind and dust.

"No. I didn't see them. But how did they get the binder 'way up there in those trees?" My voice was puzzled.

Before Dad could answer Barbe came puffing up. "Yikes! Is that thing ... up in the trees ... a binder? It looks like the wreckage of a plane." Barbe's voice held awe. "How did it get up there?"

Dad, his thumbs hooked speculatively under his overall braces, studied the situation before he spoke. "When the binder careened into those saplings rimming the poplar bush they must have bent and become a ramp for it to ride up on. It kept riding up on successively larger trees until it hit poplars too big and solid to bend, then the pin holding the evener snapped and the horses ran on without it."

We found the four horses farther into the bush. They were so thoroughly tangled they couldn't move, but still frightened enough to try to run off again if given half a chance. Miraculously none of them were hurt. Even the harness had escaped virtually intact except for one broken cross-line, two broken tugs, and a couple of belly-bands undone.

Dad's eyes narrowed as he limped back to examine the wreckage. The tautness around his mouth said he was more worried than he cared to admit. I had seen that same look the time a hail-storm had wiped us out. It had summer-fallowed cereal crops, blackened gardens, shredded shingles, damaged buildings, and indiscriminately killed so many domestic chickens and native birds that for days the smell of death hung over the land. One neighbour lost several small pigs, another a calf. We worried about a young foal, but it was okay.

"That binder's totalled," I muttered, wondering out loud if there might be any hope of buying a good second-hand machine ... and already knowing there wasn't. Not in time to finish this year's harvest.

After a few minutes of surveying what looked like a complete write-off, Dad pushed back his sweat-stained cap and straightened abruptly, as if a load had suddenly been lifted off his shoulders. "If the dealer has the parts I'll have it running again in a couple of days. Three at the most. If you girls can put the horses away I'll go in and start phoning."

I saw the start of another runaway. The hired man was heading off to do road-work, a customary way in the early years of the twentieth century for farmers to work off part of their land taxes. He had the brown mares Daphne and Daisy hitched to the low stone-box wagon with Nellie and Babe walking as wing horses. The wagon was loaded with a barrel of water, plus hay and oats for the noon feeding along with a pail and a galvanized tub for watering the horses.

Nellie and Babe were a team Dad had bought from Felix Oberg, a well-known Belgian breeder in the Amisk area. They were big, they were beautiful, and they were powerful, but Dad always maintained they didn't have half a brain between them. They caused a lot of runaways.

On this occasion the rattle of the galvanized tub may have frightened them. More likely it was just sheer hellery that made Nellie and Babe break into a run as if a devil was riding their tail.

When the hired man lost a line he knew there was no possible way he could stop them, so he bailed out in time to miss being hit by the flying water barrel and tub. The wagon itself upset while making the turn out the gate and onto a grid road, then it was no time until the wheels worked off and rolled into the bushes.

Dragging a wagon without wheels slowed the brown mares Daphne and Daisy enough to swerve the outfit off the road and into a poplar bluff. It hadn't been their idea to run in the first place, so they were glad to stop as soon as the wagon came up against the poplars, but the Belgium mares had the momentum to snap the cross-lines and continue on their merry way.

Daphne and Daisy were quickly led back to the barn. It was mid-afternoon before Nellie and Babe where found. They were eight miles from home.

Babe and Nellie were also responsible for a runaway on the seed-drill. Dad, sensing they were more skittish than usual that morning, headed the outfit down a long stretch of field before stopping to refill the seed box. When he had finished, the click of the lid snapping shut made Nellie leap and run as if someone had thrown a hornets' nest under her belly. The other horses, fed by her fear, went too.

This time Dad was ready for them. He had the drill in gear with the levers down so if they chose to tear down the field at a gallop the seed would still be going into the ground. Afterwards he laughed, "That's the fastest seeding I've ever done."

One of our hired men didn't like the Belgium mares. Albert claimed they were always lying in wait for him, trying to tramp on his toes or crowd him against the side of their stall. One day he came in for dinner madder than a grizzly with an abscessed tooth, his clothes dripping. He swore that Babe had picked him up by the shirt collar, then dropped him into the horse-trough. I giggled, but saw Dad's frown in time to bite my tongue before I would have blurted out "You got just what you deserved." Albert had never learned that with horses, as with any animals, kindness works better than brute force and a violent temper.

Babe and Nellie might be runaways, they might be skittish, but they weren't mean. I could walk up to them in the pasture and curry them all over—back legs, underbellies, tails, everywhere—without them moving. And they never stepped on my toes.

However, there came a day when Dad decided Nellie and her side-kick Babe would never be the reliable farm team he required. Consequently they were sold to a horse-buyer wanting big, good-looking Western animals for work in an Ontario logging camp. I wonder how many runaways they triggered in that province.

Paddy was a standard-bred that had been recently purchased so my sisters, Eileen and Barbara, could drive to school. When distemper hit our horses, Paddy got it worse than most, so Eileen and Mom pampered and petted him and he wasn't used all summer and autumn until the snow fell. Even then, when Dad agreed that Harvey, the current hired man and better than average with horses, could drive Paddy to town in the cutter, he wondered if perhaps he was putting the bay pony back to work too soon.

He could have saved his concern.

Paddy left the yard at a sober trot, a gait he maintained until Harvey pulled him over to let a car go by. Then something seemed to snap in his brain. He lit out after the car, paying so little attention to the reins that he was in effect pulling the cutter by his mouth. Not only would he not stop, he was gaining on a car driven by an elderly farmer who rarely exceeded the speed limit, and never looked back. In another moment Harvey would either have to swing Paddy out and pass the car (which he couldn't do on account of the high ridging of rock-hard snow on either side) or ram into its back end.

Harvey made a split-second decision. Bracing his feet against the dash-board and throwing all his weight onto one line, he dragged Paddy's head around to the left, forcing him into a deep ridging of snow. The horse floundered for a few minutes, then gave up.

At supper that night Harvey said, "I've driven horses all my life, and broken a lot of colts, but that's the first time I've ever been really scared. I still can't believe I couldn't make that pony stop."

Right then Dad decreed that Paddy was not a suitable horse for his daughters to drive to school. But as Eileen liked to ride him and he seemed quite sensible under saddle he stayed on the farm.

Eileen Kennedy and Paddy.

Paddy was as tough as railroad steel, but once Eileen and I almost finished him off.

It was during the war ... when it was patriotic to gather bleached bones to be made into fertilizer. Or bombs.

This particular Saturday promised to be dull so we Kennedy girls decided to contribute to the war effort by gathering bones. Accordingly we hitched Paddy to the

stone-boat, and with Barbe riding escort on her Shetland, Topsy, and the dog, Sniffer, trotting alongside, we
headed for the far pasture. There would be no trouble
finding lots of old bones out there.

As we were getting close to the bone-site a coyote
attracted our attention. It had seen Sniffer and seemed
to be closing in for a fight. Or maybe it was just curious.
Anyway, we were looking for some excitement so we
gave a yell and started after it. The coyote didn't turn tail
and run as we had expected, so Eileen shook out the
lines and Paddy broke into a lope that immediately
became a hard, pounding, far-reaching gallop.

The stone-boat was flying now, ricocheting off hidden rocks at every stride. Strange. I hadn't realized the
prairie wool on this quarter section hid so many rocks.
With the stone-boat bouncing about like a cork in a
wild sea, and with nothing to hang onto, it was impossible to stay on my feet, so I rolled off. I came up on my
feet in time to see Eileen throw away the lines and bale
out. The next moment Barbe fell off Topsy. When asked
why she had done that she replied somewhat tersely,
"Everyone else was falling off. I thought I'd better too."

By this time I was laughing too much to be concerned about the runaway. After all, it was only the
stone-boat. If Paddy wrecked it, so what? We could
patch it up. Paddy would run home. And no harm done.
Unless Mom saw him arrive at the barn without us—
then she would be worried. So we caught Topsy, who
had been standing nearby looking vaguely puzzled, and
sent Barbe home to tell Mom we were okay.

Eileen and I followed the stone-boat tracks until we
found where it had broken loose against a tree.

As expected, Paddy was in the barn when we got
there. Apart from a broken tug, bruises on both back

heels, and a more scared look than we thought a simple runaway seemed to warrant, he appeared none the worse for the escapade. We patched up the harness, took him out to bring the stone-boat home, and then forgot about the incident save to giggle now and then at the memory of the spectacle we must have made.

However, when I arrived home the following weekend I learned the sores on Paddy's heels had become weepy and infected, despite the care Eileen and Mom had been giving them. Still, they didn't look bad enough to cause any real concern.

Yet the horse was starting to act queer. Sometimes he walked about holding his head high, his nose pointing skyward as if he thought he was an anti-aircraft gun. When offered hay or grass he'd often just hold it in his mouth instead of eating it. He seemed to have trouble drinking too.

The next morning when Dad went out to milk he found Paddy climbing walls. He had already gone over the planks in the box stall and now he was trying to get a foothold on the barn wall itself.

There had been cases of equine sleeping-sickness reported in the district. We suspected that. But when the Vet came he took one look at Paddy and said. "That horse is already dead. He just doesn't know enough to fall over."

Intrigued by what was to him a fascinating case, the Vet finally decided Paddy had a brain fusion, probably brought on by the continual banging of his heels against the stone-boat the week before.

At a gallop Paddy's stride had lengthened and become too long for traces, which had been hitched with nothing faster than a trot in mind. It became a vicious circle. The faster he ran, the harder he hit his heels. The harder he hit his heels the faster he ran. It's lucky a trace broke and the single tree came loose when it did.

We realized now that the jolting we had blamed on the stone-boat ricocheting off rocks was caused by the lambasting given it by Paddy's frenzied heels.

The Vet left a white powder to give Paddy. He suggested we keep him quiet, put cold compresses on his head, and squirt water into his mouth to keep his tongue, which was swollen and lolling out, as moist as possible.

Thanks to Mom's nursing Paddy did recover, and from that time onward he idolized her.

I would like to say Paddy never ran away again. But it was after that episode that he ran away with Barbe and almost knocked her off by ducking under a low-hanging branch. Ever since she'd been old enough to ride him, his favourite trick had been to try to brush her off by swerving under low branches. This time he made her mad enough that she began using a severe bit on him. After that he never tried that trick again.

Once Eileen decided it would be quicker to ride Paddy bareback to the pasture than to lead him. Because she was in a hurry she didn't bother to fasten the bridle's throat-latch and Paddy, sensing it, promptly shook the bridle off. As soon as he did his head went down, his heels went up and Eileen went off … for once with nothing good to say about the horse she liked to champion.

In all the years we have spent working with horses, no one in my family has ever had an accident they couldn't walk away from.

Chapter Eight

Pompey—A New Love

By now I was a career girl, working at the Bank of Montreal and home only on weekends to ride Pompey, the Morgan mare I had bought using every carefully saved dollar from my first year's salary. The moment I'd seen the ad I had felt driven by a strange sort of compelling urgency that I *had* to have *that* Morgan filly ... the one with "some Arabian blood." It didn't matter that I would be handing over three times as much money for an unbroken three-year-old I'd not even seen a picture of than other people were paying for well-trained saddle horses. Maybe Pompey was meant to shape my destiny.

Jimmy Kennedy on the three-year-old Morgan mare, Pompey.

When the filly arrived at the livery stable in Hughenden my brother Jim agreed to ride her home. It never occurred to me that throwing a saddle on an unbroken horse, then riding her through town, might be as foolhardy as running blindfolded down precipitous mountain trails. So when Jim told me afterwards, "She was a little jumpy around town but considering she'd never been ridden before she behaved *okay*," I wasn't surprised. It was what I had expected. However, that coming from Jim was high praise. Cars, not horses, were his "thing."

The following weekend when I saw Pompey for the first time something inside me leaped. She had that special look that comes from a careful blending of blood and beauty. Jim had ridden her a couple of times during the week; now he pronounced her "broke," and she did indeed seem to be.

I named the black filly with hind socks and a stripe that spread over her nostrils Pompey because it had a nice eastern ring. I shrugged when Mom said, "But Pompey is the anglicized name for Gnaeus Pompeius Magnus, a famous Roman general, statesman and triumvir who was defeated by Julius Caesar fifty years before the birth of Christ."

Pompey would bear his name with dignity.

I lived now for weekends and Pompey. We might start the day with a gallop around the block (which in the country translates into a distance of six miles), ride six to sixteen miles in the afternoon, then home for supper and often another ride in the cool of the evening.

Those were the days before I had heard of hundred-mile endurance rides. Had Pompey competed in them I fancy she would have done rather well. She had stamina and she had heart. And she was fast.

Dad was driving the buggy with Paddy. Dad and Eileen were in the buggy, and I, wanting to see how the new horse behaved, was riding behind on Pompey. Paddy was dawdling so I decided to ride ahead. When I did he leaped and made as if to race me. Dad pulled him up, but not liking that trait in Paddy he suggested I drop back, then ride past him again. And keep doing it until Paddy got used to being passed. Sometimes Paddy would want to race, sometimes he seemed too asleep to care who went past him. Thinking he was a dead-head, and not likely to give any more trouble, I waved "ta-ta" to the folks in the buggy and rode past them again.

This time I immediately felt Pompey's muscles tense, her stride lengthen. A quick backwards glance told me a galloping horse and careening buggy was closing in on us. I didn't need to see Eileen make a wild grab for the lines—as if needing to help Dad stop Paddy—to know she thought the horse was running out of control.

But of course Paddy would stop. I'd pull Pompey over, let him go by me, and there would be nothing to race.

However, Paddy had other ideas. He had the bit in his teeth and Dad (with Eileen's help) could have been pulling on a block of concrete for all the effect the lines were having. There was a corner coming up fast and they'd never make the turn. It they attempted it, the buggy would almost certainly upset. So Dad intended to by-pass the corner and go straight ahead onto a little-used road. But he hadn't counted on Paddy's stubborn streak. The gelding had always turned that corner before and by golly he was going to turn it this time too.

Dad had the bay pony's head pulled around until it was all but touching his left side, yet his body was still travelling to the right. However, because his head was pulled off centre he swung wide into the turn and got the buggy straddling the fence, two wheels on either side. For a while the buggy flew down the fence-line, clipping off posts like chips flying from a master woodsman's axe. The snapping of each breaking post added fresh bursts of speed to the runaway.

No buggy could take much of this sort of punishment. Dad, with relief, saw a spot where the wires were sagging enough so he was able to get the buggy back onto the road again. Still Paddy ran. Another mile meant another corner. What would happen there?

Should I ride up and try to grab Paddy's head? If I did could I stop him? Or would it only spook him into causing a worse accident?

Dad called to me from the buggy, "No. You stay back. I want to get the run out of him once and for all." So Paddy was slowed for the corner, then slapped into a gallop again.

About the time Paddy seemed ready to stop a car whizzed by. That set him off again, running like a hungry greyhound after a rabbit.

The astonished driver, a car dealer, looked back, then floored the gas pedal. Ed Bell wasn't about to have a buggy pass his brand new Ford. No car salesman worth his salt wanted that sort of publicity, and certainly not Ed Bell. He was one of Ford's top salesmen.

While the trip to town set records, Paddy hadn't even worked up a good sweat. However, coming home he was content to trot like any ordinary horse. Neither cars, nor Pompey's passing him, excited any further desire to race. Hopefully he was cured.

Pompey was to be at the centre of my life for the next decade. Many horses would have hated me for asking so much of them and would have been hard to catch. Not Pompey. In all the years we owned each other the only times she walked away from me was when I rode out to get her on another horse. Then she'd toss her head and stalk off looking as cross as crabs because I wasn't riding her.

In order to catch her then I'd have to dismount and tell her she was my favourite horse and always would be. Then she'd stop and look back, her eyes throwing steel darts in a suspicious "Do you really mean it" look. Then she'd wait for me to pet her and we were friends again.

I never needed a treat, a halter or even a rope, when I walked out to the pasture to get her. A hand on her mane was all it took to lead her home. Often I just walked and she followed me. Jim said it was like magic ... as if I led her by an invisible thread.

When saddled, Pompey acted so spirited and fiery that strangers seeing her and not knowing her (or me) were amazed a young woman could handle such a bundle of fire and bounce, yet I could jump on her back out in the pasture and ride her home with no control save my voice and a hand on her mane. But it took a near-accident for me to appreciate her true worth.

She had always loved a wind-whistling gallop and when going full blast was often hard to stop ... which normally I didn't mind. But one day the road was too icy for such a reckless burst of speed, so I pulled hard to slow her and broke a line. I knew a numbing moment of near-panic. My horse was running now completely out of control on a road glistening with dangerous icy patches. If she slipped and fell we could both be killed, yet it seemed foolish to even think of jumping off, so instinctively I called "whoa." There didn't seem anything else to do.

The moment Pompey had felt the rein snap, her stride had lengthened into the sizzling good gallop she loved. Then almost immediately I sensed her indecision, felt her hesitate, even slow a little. After I said "whoa" she came to a complete stop and turned to nuzzle my boot as if telling me to hurry up, get off and fix the damn line so we can get going again.

Unlike Paddy, who was smart but sneaky, Pompey was honest and dependable through and through ... except for one idiosyncrasy. Even then there were those who said that might not have surfaced if I had been there.

If Pompey's behaviour as a saddle horse seemed too good to be true, in harness she became satanic. Dad and Jim found that out the hard way the winter day they teamed Pompey with Paddy, thinking they would make a smart team of drivers. The gelding was already broken to harness. There was no reason to expect Pompey would give them any trouble.

Yet if they had paid attention to the incendiary glint building in her eyes it might have told them turbulence was imminent. At the word "get-up" Paddy tightened his tugs. But Pompey exploded. She turned into a killer tornado gone beserk. She lunged, she reared, she bucked, she kicked, and she did it with such frenzied tenacity Dad was afraid she might kill herself. Nor did she stop fighting until her harness was broken, the sleigh-pole was cracked, her mouth was bleeding, she had a gash above one eye, and both her back legs were skinned. It was as if she saw as sacrosanct her right to remain a saddle horse, whereas working in harness was plebeian and beneath her dignity.

I went along with her decision. I hadn't been crazy about the idea either, so there was no more trying to break her to drive. Yet she'd pull the toboggan from the saddle-horn like an old pro. On winter weekends a black streak followed by a blur of misted snow flying across the field meant Pompey and I were giving someone a ride on the toboggan.

One day I walked with a rather special young man out to where the horses were pasturing more than a mile away. When we got there and I said "I guess I'll take Pompey back to the barn" his eyebrows arched in sudden surprise. "How can you? You didn't bring a halter. Or a rope."

"Oh, I don't need anything. She'll follow me. Or I can jump on her back and she'll take me home."

Hearing this, and assuming she must be a very staid and docile animal indeed, he suggested, "Then why don't we both ride her home?" What he didn't know was that Pompey had never carried double before, and I wasn't about to tell him that what he had suggested might be an open invitation for trouble. Horses who have never carried double before are usually expected to act up a bit the first time, even those properly saddled and bridled. We'd be riding Pompey bareback with absolutely no way to control her should she view being asked to carry double as demeaning as she did being driven in double harness. However, I wasn't about to admit I had concerns about how my horse might act, so I let him give me a leg up, and while I patted Pompey's neck and talked too her, he jumped on behind. She took us home as if carrying double was as natural for her as breathing in and out.

However, when we reached the yard and I told my companion that Pompey had never carried double, before his mouth dropped. He suddenly looked like someone who finds out what he thought was a harmless trinket was a ticking time-bomb.

Dad sometimes grumbled about Pompey and Paddy. He said they were trouble-makers. They led his work horses astray. When he was bringing his draft animals in from the pasture the ponies would frequently kick up their heels and gallop off, taking the rest of the herd with them.

Dear old Dad. He tolerated Pompey because he knew how important she was to me, and perhaps partly because he knew as long as I had her to come home to I wasn't apt to accept any of the Bank's offers of transfers ... which would have meant promotions and more money. Nor would I join up, as many girls were doing. With the war on I now often came home after work to help Dad with the evening chores.

My weekends were so taken up with helping Dad or riding that I had little time for the young men who periodically came to our house. Mom was secretly afraid I'd end up an old maid. So when someone began showing up who admitted he didn't like riding, and only did it if he had to, my family and friends lost no time in writing him off. "Mary will give him short shrift," they said among themselves. Little did they know that Pompey had given him her stamp of approval the day we rode her double in from the pasture, and that in time I would give him my heart.

I think both Mom and Dad were pleased when this quiet, gentle man who had the drive to make dreams happen asked to take both me and Pompey off their hands. Now for the next two years wedding plans intermingled with work and riding.

A new era was beckoning. Would a Morgan mare help shape my destiny?

Chapter Nine

Strange Behaviour

Paddy was sly and crafty, but he wasn't stupid.

One evening Mom, home alone, had gone to shut up the chickens when Paddy in a nearby paddock came hurrying over to see her. Ever since his accident he had been her shadow, but somehow this evening there seemed to be something different about him; he was acting strangely agitated. "I was sure he must be trying to tell me something," Mom told us afterwards. "Then I realized that Topsy wasn't with him. And she should have been, so I crawled through the fence to go find out why.

"Paddy was all around me like a fussy old bachelor taking his small-fry nephews to the circus for the first time. I was almost afraid he'd bump into me or step on my heels, or even knock me over."

Dusk's lilac-tinted shadows were draping the distance, fusing all images together, when Mom crested a knoll. "I could just make out Topsy lying near the fence. Something about her didn't look right.

"Hurrying closer I could see she had rolled too near to the fence. Her legs were tangled in the page-wire and in struggling to pull them free she had flipped onto her back and couldn't move. I knew I had to do something quickly, but first I had to get the wire-cutters. Without them there wasn't a hope of getting her unsnarled.

"While I was working to cut what began to look like an interminable number of wire strands, Paddy stayed right beside me, sometimes nuzzling Topsy as if assuring her 'Everything's going to be okay now,' sometimes nuzzling my hair as if exhorting me to 'hurry up can't you.'"

There is no doubt that Paddy saved his little friend's life that evening because if he hadn't alerted Mom that something was wrong, and if she hadn't understood his language, hadn't found Topsy and cut her free, by morning the pony would have been dead.

Another time Paddy and Pompey, and to a lesser degree Topsy, weren't as successful as Mom in saving a horse's life. Nevertheless, they tried in a way that was so uncanny it smacked of the supernatural.

I had come home from the office to learn that Rock, Dad's big grey Percheron gelding, had colic. Rock was subject to colic but it never seemed of any real concern because walking him so he couldn't roll for a half-hour or so was all it usually took to get him over it. However, this time Dad had turned the horses out before he realized Rock was having a colic attack. So when he came in for supper he suggested, "Mary, if you want a walk this evening how would you like to make sure Rock keeps moving for a little while?"

"Sure, Dad. Glad to. I could do with the exercise after a day in the office." It was a balmy spring evening, with the music of frogs and birds vying for twilight dominance.

I hadn't been walking behind Rock for more than a few minutes when Pompey and Paddy came to join me. As usual Topsy tagged along behind. The rest of the horses couldn't care less what I was doing; they were more interested in nipping off newly sprouting grasses.

Now when Rock showed signs of wanting to stop and roll, Paddy and Pompey, with their ears laid flat back and teeth bared, would dive towards him and get him moving again. This was bizarre behaviour for horses who normally skulked in obsequious servility if Rock threw a mean look in their direction.

The saddle horses had taken over so well that when gloaming deepened into dusk I went in, wondering how long they would continue to keep Rock moving if I wasn't there. Actually there didn't seem any need for them to continue. The big grey had passed manure, and he appeared more interested in eating now than in rolling, so obviously he was feeling better.

The first twittering of birds was promising a full-throated dawn chorus and a sleepy sun was tossing its tenuous streamers of subtle pinks and yellows above the horizon when something startled me out of a sound sleep. Struggling up in bed, I listened.

Just a couple of the horses squealing at each other, I told myself as I snuggled back down under the covers. But it came again. And again. Sharp and insistent, over-riding the other sounds of morning. There was something so urgent, so impelling in the shrill squeals that I dragged myself out of bed and over to the window. Immediately all thoughts of sleep vanished.

There, in a little draw not far from the house, spotlighted by the first rays of a new day, I witnessed a drama so extraordinary, so incredible it smacked of the supernatural.

Rock was down. On his side. The black mares, Pompey and Topsy, were circling him in slow, funereal despondency. Paddy was standing close to Rock's head as if psyching himself up for another concentrated effort of mind and muscle. As I watched, his head stretched out and he had the big Percheron's forelock gripped in his teeth. Then began a life-and-death tug-of-war as he struggled to pull the grey up onto his feet.

With feet digging in and scrambling he pulled with every muscle, every nerve, every fibre he possessed. As he did the high, shrill, urgent squeals of the mares came again and again to shatter the morning stillness, goading (or encouraging) him to still greater effort. Rock made a valiant attempt to lurch to his feet. Indeed for a moment I thought with Paddy's help he was going to make it. Instead he fell back, gave a shuddering sigh, kicked and was still.

The mares immediately stopped circling and moved closer. Now all three stood over Rock, their heads drooping, their stance dejected. Could any human hope to be mourned more eloquently?

I don't know how long I watched in spellbound fascination before they moved slowly off to join pasture mates who had shown a total disregard for what was happening.

I went back to bed, but not to sleep. I had just witnessed a drama such as few humans have been privy to seeing. It was a humbling experience.

A few months after that incident Pompey was the main player in an event that can't be explained unless horses have an intuitive sixth sense humans can't comprehend.

My black Morgan, like many mares, had a mothering instinct that surfaced whenever a new foal was born on the farm.

Flynn was a draft mare's colt who, except when nursing, spent most of his time alongside Pompey. He stayed so close to her that the easiest way to get Flynn into the barn with his mother was to lead Pompey in; then he'd follow her.

However, like all colts, Flynn had to be weaned, so when the weather turned cold he was taken off his mother, kept in the barn, and led out for water. For the first few days his mother and Pompey often ran in from the pasture to whinny to him ... calls that he soon ignored because with Dad's chore team for company and lots to eat, Pompey and his mother were no longer important to him.

As winter snow deepened and the cold intensified, the horse herd pasturing a mile from home rarely bothered to come back to the yard.

Sometime in mid-January Flynn got distemper. Dad thought he was over it; then a sudden relapse in February took his life. The morning he died Mom, looking out her kitchen window, was startled to see Pompey come galloping in from the pasture despite a bitter wind, floundering through deep, hard-crusted drifts that would almost hold her up but not quite. She came by herself, which was highly unusual, but even stranger than that was the way she ran back and forth watching the barn door and whinnying on a high note that had about it an almost hysterical urgency. Then she would stop, head up, ears pricked. Listening. For what? An answering whinny? Flynn's message that he was alive and well?

It didn't come. But she didn't give up hoping until afternoon shadows were lengthening into an early dusk. Then, reluctantly, she headed back to the pasture to rejoin the other horses.

She came again the next day, and the next, staying for progressively shorter periods. Now her whinnying held a resigned, despondent note.

What caused her unprecedented behaviour? An animal instinct? A premonition? The calling of spirit to spirit? Something that defies human understanding?

Chapter Ten

Rocky Ridges

In late December 1946, I married Clarence Burpee, the man of my choice, and we moved to our new home on a section of land near the Battle River that we aptly named Rocky Ridges. It was ten miles from both Hughenden and Amisk.

In early January 1947 Clarence's new John Deere Model D tractor arrived in Amisk. It had come by train from Lethbridge, because that was the only place in Alberta that had one available. (New tractors, cars, farm machinery, even stoves and washing machines, were hard to get in those first few years following the war.)

The day that Clarence went to Amisk to bring his tractor home I continued on to my parents' place and after a visit with them I rode Pompey to our new home at Rocky Ridges.

My first few months of married life were largely spent chasing neighbours' cows out of our crops. Pompey and I got lots of exercise.

Then I got pregnant and the doctor forbade riding. However, I risked one final ride when prairie hillsides were redolent with the fragrance of silver willow in full bloom. (The smell of silver willow in June still brings back nostalgic memories of a forbidden ride, and a first pregnancy.)

With a baby girl to keep me house-bound, and a husband putting in long hours doing field work for ourselves as well as for neighbouring farmers, there were few chances the next spring for me to ride, so I welcomed the times our cattle had to be moved.

One day at noon I set out on Pompey to take them to our pasture near the river. It wasn't far. Only a mile.

"It shouldn't take long," I smiled at Clarence. "I'll be back before you finish eating." I knew he was anxious to get out to the field again because he and the hired man, Peter Prost, were hoping to keep the outfit running 24 hours a day (an impossible goal). Besides, if I was gone too long the baby would be awake and hungry.

I hadn't expected a gate into one of Louis Delange's rough and hilly pastures to be open, so I wasn't watching for it as I should have been. But the cows saw it and were through it before I could stop them. Then, frisking and bucking, they galloped gaily off as if congratulating themselves for having done something very clever.

Ordinarily it would have been easy enough to head them off and get them back. Except crowding this gate was a heavy stand of trees so dense cows could squeeze between them or duck under their low-hanging branches—a rider couldn't. I had to gallop around the entire bluff, and it was a large one, to get ahead of animals convinced that having discovered Utopia they must explore it immediately. Consequently, each time I had the herd almost back to the gate they'd kick up their heels, lower their heads, crash through the dense undergrowth, race into the trees, and high-tail it down one of the many ill-defined, meandering cow paths like a covey of shot-at partridges. In heavy brush I couldn't stop them.

Each time they escaped into the trees I had to make a wide detour to bring them back, but they would always be off again. Finally I got off and left Pompey standing where she would block them from escaping down one path, while I raced hunchbacked between crowding poplars and sagging willows to try to head off critters already escaping down a dozen other cow-trails.

It was an exercise in futility. There were too many crowding trees to squeeze between; too many low-slung branches to take malicious swipes at a face already stinging from a crisscross of welts; too many rotting logs and gnarled old roots hidden among last year's decaying leaves and this spring's innocuous wood violets to trip me; too many brambles to tear at my clothes, scratch my arms and legs and face; too many dense thickets of saskatoon and chokecherry bushes I couldn't wriggle through.

It was so hot the horizon fused with the sky. Sweat dripped in my eyes, blurred my vision. It lathered Pompey's black coat a dirty white.

Even among the trees there was no relief from the arrogant blaze of the sun. No breeze whispered through the latticework of leaves to bring even a moment's respite from the unrelenting heat. And always there were mosquitoes. Thousands of blood-hungry mosquitoes fighting to stake their claim wherever they could find even a modicum of exposed skin. Be it human or equine.

Worse than the brambles, the heat, the mosquitoes, and the frustration, there was mounting worry. I had been gone far too long. The baby would be awake. My husband would be walking the floor with her, darting anxious glances between clock and road.

He would be picturing me thrown, unconscious, flies clustering around my half-open mouth, ants crawling into my ears. Perhaps I had a broken leg, but Pompey wouldn't leave me. Or it could be Pompey. She had stepped into a badger hole and broken her leg.

A whole army of possible tragedies marched through my mind, each one more grisly than the one preceding it. I began feeling like a martyr. Yet Clarence knew, as I did, that unless my black mare tripped and fell there was little chance I'd get hurt. Pompey was a horse you couldn't fall off because she wouldn't allow it. If she sensed her rider was slipping she always managed to get her body back under you again.

Despite the grisly array of imagined calamities, the thing that very nearly did do us in wasn't among them.

I'd often heard Clarence and neighbouring ranchers with pastures adjacent to the Battle River talk about having to pull critters out of soap-holes. Few survived. The animals that got sucked in and stuck were almost always new to the district; those raised in the area were rarely a problem. They seemed to be born with the instinct to keep away from dangerous muskegs. Pompey was new to the district.

I was hot, hurting, and humiliated that the cows were getting the best of me. Clarence, anxious to get back to the field, would be in a worry-stew. Baby Heather hadn't been fed. She'd be awake and screaming. But I hated to give up.

There was what I took to be a dried slough bottom, grown up now to grass and weeds, in a small opening between two poplar bluffs. If I crossed that it ought to bring me out ahead of cows already crashing through underbrush in their latest bid for freedom. Maybe this time I'd get lucky.

Pompey worked her way out of the trees we were in, then lit out for the grassy draw at a sizzling gallop, determined to get across it before the cows could escape into the second bush.

It happened with the suddenness of death. Pompey was floundering in slimy, squelching muskeg. The horrible slurping sounds of mud sucking her still deeper, mingled with the whistle of air escaping from a terrified animal's over-taxed lungs, shattered the silence as the ooze of brackish muskeg closed around her.

My mind was a swirling mass of indecision. Momentum had already carried the floundering mare too far out into the flaccid morass I'd mistaken for a dry slough-bottom. Yet it seemed our best, and perhaps only hope was to try to go back. However, I knew that for a horse to turn in this bog would take a near-miracle. Once an animal went down it could never get up. Not without help. For me to attempt to pull Pompey out alone would be like a gopher trying to pull an elephant. I'd have to run home for Clarence and the tractor. What if we didn't get back in time? Horses die quickly in muskeg.

While these thoughts were tumbling through my mind, Pompey was taking matters into her own hands.

Heaving and straining, eyes wild with fright, the breath torn from her tortured lungs in great gasping sobs, she struggled to turn and get back to firm ground. As she fought the prehensile ooze with terrible determination, her hooves were throwing such a barrage of mud skyward that we were both covered in a blanket of filth and slime.

She was nearly up to her forearms in an undulating, deceiving, grass-coated morass of bog-jelly-ooze that was determined to grab her, drag her down, claim her for its victim. She was just as determined to escape it. She floundered and fought her way back towards firm ground with a wild and courageous glint in her eyes.

While this was happening my mind screamed, "Bail out! Without you she might have a chance." But my body was as unresponsive as if it was frozen in an Arctic glacier. While Pompey's hooves were flinging barrages of mud skyward I was too petrified to move. And I'm not proud of that.

When the mare finally did reach firm ground she was blowing in such heaving, tearing gasps and trembling so violently I was afraid I'd killed her.

The damn cows could go to blazes; we were going home. If she could get there.

By the time I'd wiped the mud from her nostrils and from around her eyes and led her slowly up the path and out of the trees she was breathing almost normally again. In fact she seemed quite recovered. So I remounted, and when I did she promptly broke into a trot which I felt guilty about allowing but didn't check because I knew how worried Clarence would be about me. In fact I was surprised he hadn't come looking for me. And that started me worrying about him. And the baby.

Pompey's trot became a gallop.

I threw myself from the saddle and tore up the steps, expecting to be met at the door by an anxious husband asking, "Princess, are you all right? What took you so long?"

Instead I was met by utter silence. Nothing. Cold, raw panic tore at my mind as I raced across the kitchen. At the bedroom door my mouth dropped in stunned disbelief, my body sagging like a sack of dry chicken feathers. I leaned weakly against the door jamb. And swore. Which is something I don't normally do.

How could he sleep like that? Damn it! What the hell did he mean by sleeping … when he should be pacing the floor? Why wasn't he worrying over what had happened to me? That was the very least he could have done. Yet here he was, looking as relaxed and peaceful as baby Heather, who slept snuggled in the crook of his arm.

Whereas my face was crisscrossed with welts that felt as if they were being poked with red hot pincers each time another trickle of salty sweat slid into them. My knee hurt. The bad one. I'd tripped over a hidden root and taken a hard tumble. My arms were scratched and bleeding, my body was an itching torment of mosquito bites. I was muddier than a hog in a wallow, and so sweaty my jeans stuck and chafed. The cows had beaten me. I had fretted myself into a dither ... worrying that Clarence would be worrying about me. Worst of all, I had almost killed Pompey.

And here was my husband, clean, cool and completely relaxed, sleeping as if he didn't have a care in the world. Damn him!

I stomped off to the barn. To take care of Pompey. And have a good cry.

That evening, when both I and the weather had cooled off considerably, Clarence went with me to help get the cows to their proper pasture. This time they walked out so easily Pompey and I could have done it on our own.

My sister Barbara, a nurse in training at Edmonton's Royal Alexander hospital, never missed a chance to come out and ride Pompey. After Mom and Dad moved to town she brought Paddy out and left him in our pasture. So now when she came home we could ride together. Provided I had someone to baby-sit our growing family, Heather and baby Terry Lee.

Sometimes we rode across country to where Clarence was doing custom-tilling on land not far from the Battle River. One day after bringing him a cold drink we headed home by way of the river road. The day was hot enough to fry bacon. An old swimming hole in a shady bend of the river looked illicitly tempting. We didn't have bathing suits, but what the heck.

It was two miles to the nearest house, owned by a bachelor known to his neighbours as Cadet. He was a hound to work. He didn't visit around the district much, so it seemed highly improbable he would be wasting time near the swimming hole today.

So why were we hesitating?

It only took a moment to tie the horses in the bush, duck out of our clothes, and drop into the river.

It was fun splashing about, until we realized the sound we had been hearing in the distance was no longer in the distance. It was close and coming closer.

"Holy Cow! It's Cadet!"

The Frenchman was mowing the hay-field directly above us. I could see the ears of his team and the top of his battered felt hat through the screening of bushes that stuck out of the river-bank above us like scrawny toothpicks.

To scramble up the other side now and race for our clothes was suicide. It couldn't fail to attract his attention. Any movement ... or sound.... and he'd be over to investigate. We hugged the river-bank, hoping our horses wouldn't whinny and that Cadet wouldn't look down. If we'd been bank swallows we would have crawled into one of their holes.

Barbe looked like a tightly coiled spring ready to burst into giggles, but I mouthed a threat at her that choked off so much as a snicker until Cadet had moved well on around the field. Then our breath burst out like the swoosh of white water escaping dams. Speculative titters tinkled the stillness. What would we, or he, have done had he looked down and seen us? Fortunately that was a question we hadn't had to answer.

We headed home, promising never to tell Mom or Dad about this adventure. But we did tell Clarence.

Cadet thought I was special. Blizzards had blocked the side roads, making it hard even for sleighs to get through some of the drifts. Nor had we seen Cadet ride by, and that seemed unusual because he usually went by our house every week to visit the Prosts, a large French family living north of us who picked up groceries and mail for him whenever any of them went into Amisk. They hadn't seen anything of Cadet either.

That started us worrying. What if something had happened to him? Living alone as he did on an isolated road, miles from the nearest neighbour (we were the closest at two miles plus), with no telephone, and a hundred cows depending on him for food and water ... he could be in big trouble. Clarence offered to stay with our two little girls if I wanted to ride down to check on him.

While my husband was saddling Pompey for me I pulled a pair of his shrunken wool underwear on under my jeans, and got into my snow pants and parka. Then, with a dozen freshly-baked buns in a bag, a scarf wrapped around my face and buffalo-hide mitts, furred and gauntleted, on my hands, I climbed onto Pompey and started out.

Cold drifting in from the high Arctic had settled heavily over a land that groaned and snapped under its weight. Days of continuous winds racing with relentless rhythm across the fields had pounded swirling snow into rock-hard drifts. The roads were heavy going, even for a saddle horse as athletic as Pompey.

A few orphan snowflakes floating silently down peppered the mare's black mane. Somewhere a woodpecker hammered a tree. When a lone magpie flapped across my vision and disappeared I remembered the Irish superstition. "One for sorrow. Two for joy. Three for a girl. Four for a boy." Dad always had a puckish grin and a mischievious sparkle in his blue eyes as he recited that verse to us when we saw magpies. But if there was only one bird he always acknowledged it by respectfully touching his cap …. He said that would break the evil spell. There was no sense taking chances.

The magpie I had seen was long gone. And I hadn't touched my cap. Dad said women didn't need to, but now I wished I had. My voice sounded strained as I patted Pompey's neck, murmuring, "It's not much farther now."

Grisly thoughts had begun flooding my mind. What would I do if Cadet didn't answer when I knocked? Should I open his door, and walk in? If I did what would I find? Maybe I should look around outside first? But where? He could be anywhere. Maybe hurt? Or dead? What if I found him partly eaten by coyotes? I wished Clarence had come with me.

When I came in sight of Cadet's buildings some of the apprehension left me like a great swoosh of escaping breath. Smoke was coming from the chimney. At least he must be alive. Getting closer I could see his cattle had been fed recently. I knocked on the door with a lighter heart.

When Cadet opened the door and saw me standing there, a great welcoming smile flooded his face and a second later he was pulling me into his kitchen as if I was a harbinger of spring. Or maybe an angel who had exchanged gauzy wings for snow-suit and parka.

Besides suffering from a severe case of winter loneliness he had been, and still was, fighting a flu bug that left him too exhausted after the daily chore of feeding cattle to want to bother riding for help. Especially as he was a man with too proud and independent a spirit to want to admit that he might need help. Instead he had been trying to tough it out, promising himself if he survived this winter he'd never spend another winter alone.

The next spring when the fish were running in the Battle River he brought Clarence and me a big bag of what I thought must be some sort of water-snake. They were long, black and sinuous, and they had no scales. They looked so repulsive I intended to throw them out as soon as Cadet left, until he said, "No. De ling. De taste real good. You cook, you see." So I did. To my surprise Cadet's ling were some of the best-tasting fish I've ever eaten.

True to his word, Cadet went back to France that spring and returned with a pretty little bride. She couldn't speak English; my French was negligible. We visited anyway.

Pompey had her first foal when she was eighteen. It was sired by Boots, a Welsh stallion we owned for a while. Boots had a crooked hind leg, broken when he was a colt. Despite this, he had won a lot of the local races in his heyday.

Somewhere in his colourful background, however, he had learned to get down and crawl under fences, so he soon went to someone with more need of a pony.

Nevertheless, despite his bad habits, Boots had quite a bit going for him, so we had big hopes for Pompey's foal, Nifty.

Nifty turned out to be a good enough pony, but he lacked that little bit extra we had expected from a mare like Pompey. However, I had some rides on Nifty I'll never forget.

Rocky Ridges had been a good first home but its hills and rocky soil made farming difficult, so when an opportunity arose to buy a farm a mile from Hughenden we had jumped at the chance. Not only was it closer for our children to attend school, but also we could get our farm electrified so we could have the convenience of electric lights and refrigeration, something that didn't seem likely to happen in the farther-out districts for many years.

After we moved, our closest neighbour was a loquacious braggart who boasted his black thoroughbred was the fastest thing on hooves. But a bit hard to catch. The day the animal got loose in a half-section of silver willow and sand dunes his owner couldn't get within a horn-blast of him, so I offered to chase him back on Nifty.

The pitying look the man shot me from under the overhang of craggy brows said I had about as much chance of doing that as pulling down the moon. However, what was there to lose? He shuffled condescendingly, worked his mouth into a benign smile, and asked, "How soon can you start?"

*Cheaper by the half-dozen! Or is Nifty wondering "Why me?"
The riders on Nifty from left to right are Terry Lee Degenhardt,
her sister Heather, Joan Wall, her brother David, Joe and George
Volk. Mrs. George (Margaret) Wall is holding Nifty, her two
younger children Patricia and Kathleen stand beside her.*

To tell the truth I wasn't all that confident about the outcome of this venture myself. Pompey would have been different. But Nifty? He'd never shown much enthusiasm for speed.

When the thoroughbred saw me closing in on him he tossed a disdainful look back over his shoulder and lit out at a ground-covering trot. Nifty broke into a gallop. The black's trot quickly turned to a pounding gallop that seemed a clincher to leave us wallowing in his dust.

It was then Nifty's ears flew back and his legs locked into racing gear. He sailed across blow-outs, jumped rocks, crashed through brambles, dodged bushes, and slithered between gnarled old silver willows. It was a wild, mad, marvellous gallop. And we were gaining on the runaway.

Unexpectedly the fire went out of the thoroughbred. He stopped, blowing like a winded marathon racer, and waited, head down and beaten, while his halter was slipped in place.

That was the autumn I was riding Nifty from Gango Ranch to Rocky Ridges, and leading Pompey. We would need both horses out there tomorrow when we would be rounding up the cattle and bringing them home. Earlier that summer we had moved to the new property near Hughenden, which we named Gango Ranch, and now with freeze-up imminent the cattle must be driven the twelve miles from Rocky Ridges, where they pastured, to Gango Ranch.

Tomorrow would be the first of what would become more than fifty years of semi-annual cattle drives between our Rocky Ridges and Gango ranches. Unfortunately tomorrow's was to be momentous in a sad and sobering way.

In early afternoon before the actual cattle drive I was

taking the horses to Rocky Ridges so they would be out there and ready for an early start the next day.

My thoughts were on tomorrow's drive. How would a range herd who had spent their life pasturing river hills, seeing nothing but the occasional motor vehicle, react to the roar of highway traffic? Even stepping on pavement would be a new experience for them. As would crossing railroad tracks, and facing the hustle and bustle of a town noisy with yappy dogs and boisterous kids.

The shrill scream of a train whistle interrupted my thoughts. Not wanting to reach the crossing until the train had rushed past, I pulled both horses to a walk. I wasn't sure how Nifty would react to a train. Like the cattle, he had been raised far from the sights and sounds of trains.

Most of my attention was on Nifty, but I was aware the train had flashed past the elevators. For a fleeting second, as one sees something in a flare of lightning, I saw an old car rattling towards the crossing before it was wiped from view by the onrushing train.

Strange how preoccupation dulls the senses.

I saw the car. I should have known immediately it and the train were on a collision course. Even the screech of twisted, tortured metal and the scream of hastily applied brakes didn't register. It wasn't until I noticed what looked like a heap of scrap-iron being pushed ahead of the cow-catcher that something in my brain clicked. Good God! There had been an accident.

I dug Nifty in the ribs and reached the engine just as the engineer, looking stunned and ghastly, climbed down, muttering through clenched teeth, "… I couldn't stop. There wasn't time." Then he sat on the bank, hid his face in his hands, and sobbed. Others who were arriving now helped pull the wreckage off the engine.

There didn't seem much point in my staying longer. There was nothing anyone could do. Victor Twigg, an area farmer, was dead. Dad would be stunned. He and Victor had worked together on the Bisset school board for years.

I rode slowly towards Rocky Ridges, no longer conscious of the autumn colours or the balmy warmth of this last fling of Indian Summer.

The next summer Nifty tried to finish me off. Well, perhaps he hadn't tried. It was an accident.

I was riding range-land south of us when I chanced on the owner trying to drive stray horses off his property with a pick-up truck. He was glad of my offer of help. But as it turned out I gave him more trouble than help.

Nifty lit out after the horses at a gallop. But almost immediately he crumpled, did a somersault that hurled me ahead of him, then caught up with me as he flipped head over heels above me. If there are miracles, surely one happened that day. Had the saddle horn gouged into me instead of the ground (and it came frighteningly close to doing so) I wouldn't be writing this. As it was, some part of Nifty did land on me, but fortunately there is more give to horse-flesh than there is to a saddle horn.

I was half stunned. My leg hurt so badly I didn't argue when Vern said, "Get in. I'm driving you home." He tied Nifty behind. When we got within sight of our house I began insisting, "I'm *okay* now. I can ride the rest of the way ... if you'll help me on. "

"No damn way I will. You've had a bad spill."

"Vern. I tell you I'm *okay*; I can ride. Believe me. Besides if Clarence sees you bringing me home he'll be scared I'm badly hurt. I don't want him thinking that. Besides, I've never had a fall I couldn't ride away from.

Don't make me break that record. Come on, Vern. Please."

So Vern helped me onto Nifty and I rode the last half mile up to the house.

But when little Terry Lee raced to meet me shouting, "Mummy! Mummy! Gimmee a ride!" I began wondering if perhaps it had been stupid to turn down the neighbour's offer. Every bone I had, and some I wished I didn't have, hurt. I had to clench my teeth and concentrate on not blacking out when I eased out of the saddle and shoved Terry Lee up into it. Walking ... hobbling, more accurately ... and that done by clutching the saddle leathers ... was sheer agony.

Looking back, I wonder why I didn't just yell for help and let someone else put Nifty away. I suppose there's more than a bit of my father's Irish stubbornness in me.

When I finally made it to the house Clarence took one look at me and demanded, "What happened to you?" Without waiting for an answer he picked me up and gently carried me to our bed, then stood staring down at me as I tried to tell him I really wasn't hurt. Not much anyway.

The outcome of that adventure was that I spent several weeks on crutches and as many more hobbling around with a cane.

When I was feeling up to it Clarence and I went back to the site of the accident to try to discover the reason for Nifty going down as he had. We found absolutely nothing. No half-hidden hole, no concealed wire, not even any rough ground. I knew now I could never gallop Nifty again and be confident there wouldn't be a similar accident. A saddle horse unsafe at a gallop was no use to me.

Nifty was traded to a man in Montana who needed a reliable horse. A horse that would amble sedately down picturesque bridle trails as part of a saddle string ridden by tourists imagining this was "the Wild West."

In trade for Nifty we got five Mexican burros, which our girls and their friends had fun riding until they were sold. But we kept Perky, a filly burro, thinking that in a few years she would be nice for Roderick, our baby son, to ride.

By this time Heather was riding our pony stallion Pablo. Terry Lee had taken to Lady, a tiny Shetland mare. The bigger Shetlands, Roxy and Rilla, were occasionally pressed into service to accommodate youthful visitors to the ranch.

With eight or ten Shetlands, plus a team of lively work horses that I liked to drive on the hayrake, and of course Pompey, I should have been content. But I wasn't. An Arabian stallion had come to Vermilion and I desperately wanted to get a foal from him and Pompey.

Pompey was bred to him but she was now well up in her twenties and there was no foal. The stud fee could be applied against another breeding, but we had no suitable mare.

Pompey, with her small percentage of Arabian blood, had whetted my appetite for a purebred. If we were buying a mare anyway, I reasoned, why not go whole hog and get a purebred? Provided we could find one for sale in Canada at a price we could afford. At that time there were fewer than 240 registered Arabians in all of Canada.

Clarence, knowing how important horses were to me and how I had dreamed of owning an Arabian even before I knew there were any in Canada, encouraged me.

"Go for it!"

A year later we made a trip to British Columbia to pick up Shasta, a mare whose dam, Guda, had been bred by Colonel Dickinson at the Travellers Rest Stud in Tennessee. The Colonel had imported Guda's parents, Czubuthan and Przepiorka, from Poland, where they had excelled on that country's race tracks and in the parenting of great progeny. Our hopes ran high.

Pompey, the mare I had bought so long ago because of her 'little bit' of Arabian blood, had fulfilled her destiny and had started me on mine. I was beginning a lifetime love affair with Arabians.

Chapter Eleven

Khem—The Stuff Dreams Are Made Of

Why didn't the damn man unlock the barn door?

It wasn't the bite of an Arctic wind that had me fidgeting like a thoroughbred at Woodbine's starting gate. It was excitement. I wanted to see *our* stallion ... not hear how many big-whig Calgarians stabled their horses in this man's barn. I gave Clarence a sly dig in the ribs. If he wouldn't appear so darned interested it might help.

Months earlier Arabian breeder Jeanette Morrill, owner of Wyoming's prestigious Bear Claw Ranch, had sent me Khem's picture and his pedigree. The picture, a side view, showed a good-looking dark chestnut yearling colt with three stockings, and because Shasta had a star I supposed he had one too. But it was the extended pedigree that was the real clincher. I didn't know much about Arabian bloodlines then, but I did know that Khem's close-up pedigree read like a who's who of world-famous Arabian progenitors. So we bought the colt on the strength of a pedigree and a picture. And that had triggered a flurry of mutterings among family and friends: "Mary has always been horse-crazy ... I credited Clarence with having more sense...."

Last night our colt had arrived in Calgary and now we were about to see him for the first time. My hands felt clammy. I shoved them deeper into my jacket's ample pockets and shivered nervously. What if we really were a bit crazy?

As the door slid open the warmth of the barn and the smell of horses reached out to me like a calming wave. A chorus of nickers filled the air. Forty heads turned to greet us from as many box stalls lining either side of a long alley-way.

My eyes flew over the faces. Then stopped, riveted to one animal. That animal's head stood out from all the others like a diamond in a tray of pebbles. Khem was temporarily forgotten.

"OH! What a gorgeous head!" My voice rang with sheer ecstasy. "That one has *got* to be an Arabian."

There was such charisma, such radiance, such ... such .... Even to this day I don't know how to properly describe it. That face had *everything*.

I moved trance-like towards pricked ears, tiny and exquisite above a face with an off-centre white stripe slip-sliding down to the right nostril of a tea-cup muzzle. It was a head of extreme refinement, from which eyes like great dark pools of intelligence were watching me.

Suddenly an amused voice at my elbow broke the trance. "Well, Ma'am. That's your horse. And he's a beaut."

"But ... but ... I didn't know he looked like that. I ... I mean ... I thought he had a star. His picture didn't show a white stripe. You see, we never really saw him." I was beginning to feel like a complete idiot.

"Well, Ma'am, if you folks can buy them like that sight-unseen how about buying one for me? That colt's as good as they come."

"Well, we had seen Khem's older brother. You must know Ramose? He's that grey Arabian here in Calgary who has become the horse to beat at shows throughtout the province. He's been doing well in both halter and performance classes. Anyway, all the Bear Claw horses seem to be so highly regarded we didn't think we could go wrong by choosing Khem. Could we?" The words came tumbling out as if there was a need to justify what we had done both to myself and to this man.

My thoughts flew back to the day my husband suggested, "Maybe we should get an Arabian stallion. Then we won't need to take Shasta away every year to be bred."

Hearing that should have sent me soaring on a heaven-sent sunbeam, but it didn't. I knew how I had to dig in my heels to hang onto Gay Boy at breeding time. If I had that much trouble leading a 43-inch Shetland stallion, an Arabian sire bursting with fire and potency would have me spending a lot of time dangling helplessly on the centrifugal end of his halter shank.

However, when Clarence agreed to handle the stallion at breeding time, the search for a suitable mate for Shasta was on. Always with my husband's admonition ringing in my ears: "Don't choose a stallion because you think he's a bargain. Go for the one you honestly believe has the breeding, the disposition and the conformation you want, a top-of-the-line sire that will outlast the fads that come and go. If I know you, whatever horse we get will be around for a long time, so don't settle for anything but the best."

On that drive home from Calgary I felt confident we had done just that.

Khem was still too young to ride but Clarence started leading him, saddled and bridled, around the yard. He accepted that so quickly my husband decided the colt was ready to begin carrying "things." Now when the reins were tied back to the horn, three empty five-gallon tin grease pails hung from the saddle leathers.

Khem calmly carried the pails bumping against his sides, and sometimes clanging against each other, as if doing it was as routine as breathing.

Khem, the horse who made dreams come true.

If it hadn't been for the overnight skiff of snow it wouldn't have happened. Clarence would have seen the slope was covered in a blanket of sheer ice and kept Khem away from it. As it was, the moment the stallion stepped onto the slope his feet shot out from under him so fast he couldn't save himself. He fell hard. The clattering and clanging of the pails as they hit the ground made enough racket to quicken the dead, and brought me racing to the window to see what was going on.

Perhaps Khem's fall put extra strain on the cinch. Perhaps it was his lurching and scrambling to regain his feet that broke it. Even so, if the lines hadn't been tied to the horn, the saddle could have flopped back down onto the ground and that would have been the end of it. As it was, when Khem scrambled to his feet, everything—saddle and pails—were dangling from his bridle.

Any horse, even the quietest, could be excused if it reared away in fright from something so foreign, so startling—fright that would mushroom into panic as the saddle and its clanging appendages flopped crazily about his head like giant pendulums gone mad. There would be no escaping them. It would be enough to send any creature racing in mindless terror towards its own destruction.

Khem was no dead-head. He was full of fire and zest. The sort of horse artists have immortalized and poets eulogized down through the ages. He was so regal, he moved with such easy grace, that when Clarence led him around the yard I liked to stand at the window to watch.

Today I was petrified. It was as if I was witnessing my own execution. Cold, terrifying panic clawed at my throat, strangled my tongue. Khem was down, lurching to his feet now, but there was something terribly wrong. The saddle, and the pails tied to it, were swinging drunkenly from his bridle. His mouth would be lacerated. He would become a whirling, fear-crazed tornado. Clarence would never be able to hold him. These thoughts screamed through my mind like maddened ghost riders lashing their startled mounts across a blood-stained sky.

Then my mouth came foolishly agape. I stared spellbound as Khem went back down on one knee and lowered his head until the saddle and pails once again rested on the ground. He knelt there, waiting quietly until Clarence was able to untie the reins and drag the saddle aside.

Then he got up as if nothing untoward had happened.

Wow! We realized now that Khem had those qualities horsemen throughout the world like to dream about.

In late February Clarence came in grinning like a Halloween pumpkin. "I think Khem could be taught to handle cattle. You know, like a Border Collie. He seems to have a natural instinct for it. I took him with me on a long rope today and he knew exactly what to do."

"Granted, Khem is no ordinary horse," I snorted, "but I can't quite imagine him obeying voice commands like "sit," "heel," "stay," and so forth. Mind you, I'm not saying he isn't smart. But really, isn't that expecting a little too much? Anyway, I plan to start riding him next week. Then we'll work cattle for you."

I wouldn't have sounded so confident had I been able to glimpse the future.

"Happy anniversary, Mom. I'm expecting you and Dad to come for supper. Nothing fancy, though. Not like we had for you last year on March 2nd. But then that was your fiftieth. Hey! I'd better go. Clarence has come in, and … ? And … !"

I didn't need a second look to know something must be very wrong. There was a stricken bleakness about my husband's haggard face as he struggled to make his words sound normal.

"Khem has hurt his eye. You'd better call the Vet." He spoke with such controlled calm it had an ominous ring.

"Hurt his eye? How? He was all right before breakfast. Is it bad?"

I should have known my husband was hedging, trying to break the news lightly. But I heard only, "He's snagged it on something. It looks bad."

Snagged? My mind said snags weren't much to get het up about. If I had a dollar for every time a horse got itself snagged on something….

Then I saw Khem. And the bottom dropped right out of my world.

Dear God! This was no snag. This was more like a knife blade had gouged out the eyeball and left it hanging by a thread.

The Vet? Would he be able to ...? There was so much blood ... Oh God! It looked awful .... Why didn't the damn Vet get here? ... do something ... anything .... say it wasn't as bad as it looked .... Maybe the eye could be saved?

I don't know how long I stayed with Khem, not sure who was comforting whom, but eventually I had to run to the house to check that the kids were okay.

It only took a few minutes to check on them (Clarence had gone to feed the cattle), and to phone Mom that Khem was hurt. Could they go to Barbe's for their anniversary supper?

The racket coming from Khem's stall as I raced back towards the barn plunged my stomach into a twisted knot. Pain must be driving him wild. Another thought zapped my brain like forked lightning. Pain can sometimes turn docile animals into crazed killers.

Would Khem attack me? I didn't think so. But even if he didn't purposely savage me, it sounded as if he was throwing himself around so recklessly it would be like walking into a pen with a rhinoceros. He could crush me against the wall without meaning too. Pumping adrenalin forced my legs still faster.

As I eased myself into his stall my mind hovered close to the panic button. What if something did happen? I had three young children ... and a husband.

"Easy, Khem boy. It's me. I'm back." The stallion turned in his pain-goaded pacing and came towards me, an almost inaudible whicker quivering his delicate nostrils. The next moment I had my arms around his neck, my face buried in the mane that flamed a brilliant red against the purple sheen of his liver-chestnut coat.

Oh, dear God! Why did this have to happen to Khem? A horse who could have had the whole world at his feet.

Blood ran with relentless rhythm from what had been the window of his soul. It trickled down, spread out, staining his white stripe a ghastly red. Deep burning anger poured over me. I clung to him and cried.

Tears and blood dripped together, falling in soft plops onto the straw. Then a velvet muzzle gently nudged my shoulder. Was he telling me, "Hey, stop your blubbering. It's my eye that's hurting"?

As long as I was with Khem he stood quietly. If I had to leave, even if only for a moment, he grew restless again.

After what seemed like an eternity the Vet's car two-wheeled it into the yard. When he saw the mess that had been Khem's eye he let go with every swear word known to man and some that he invented on the spot. It was criminal that such an accident should happen to so promising a colt.

The sight was gone. Hopelessly, irreparably gone. If Khem didn't lose the vision in his other eye as well, we could consider ourselves lucky. And there was a very grave concern infection might claim his life. At the very best he would live out his days horribly disfigured.

Khem, the horse with eyes so big, so dark, so full of fire and soul and gentleness, the horse whose head had been outstanding in a breed whose hallmark is beautiful heads, was doomed to go through life so blemished people would turn away from him in loathing.

I'm not one to cry a lot. But I cried that day.

Clarence, as devastated as I, tried to comfort me.

And I him. But it wasn't easy. The only thing we could think of that could have been worse was if it had happened to one of our children.

In the days that followed we did a Sherlock-Holmes on Khem's corral, looking for a protruding nail, some sharp object that could have done the injury. And came up with nothing.

Then another thought hit me like a whiplash. While we were eating breakfast on that fateful day ... a day so black it will remain forever burned into my memory ... a gate had come open between Khem and a pen of steers. One of those steers had horns.

Could it be that Khem's enthusiasm for chasing cows had cost him his sight? Had the one horned animal in the bunch swung its head and hooked out his eye? Clarence thought it improbable ... yet we had found nothing else that could have done it.

For now our main concern was whether Khem would live. Would he sire even one crop of foals? For him to go down to oblivion without having left any of his own excellence for posterity was too dreadful to think about.

Yet to Khem that was never a problem. He wasn't one to go easily into defeat. He had a destiny to fulfill. And by all the great horses in his pedigree, he'd fulfill it until the gods on Mount Olympus decreed the time had come to claim him for their own.

He made liars of those who came to look, and having seen cried doom. "Damn shame he lost that eye. You know of course, Mary, that you'll never be able to ride him now. A one-eyed horse is useless around cattle. Unsafe to ride under any circumstances. He'll be spooky as hell. Apt to lash out and nail you the moment something startles him." Then they would go away shaking their heads.

And I would pet Khem on his blind side and he would turn to me as if agreeing that such talk was stupid.

Before Khem was two, and just three months after his injury, I rode him on his first of many cattle drives. I knew taking him was an open invitation for trouble. The night before the drive I tossed and turned. Was it crazy? Should I ride an older, more experienced horse?

Clarence said, "Don't worry Princess. Khem can do it"

But wasn't it asking a lot of a young, untried horse? It isn't easy to herd range cows and their frisky calves across a railway track, a paved highway bristling with traffic, through a corner of town redundant with dogs, kids, *and* unfenced lawns. Then down twelve dusty miles of road beside fields and pastures, where, if resident bulls didn't come roaring over to give us trouble, then the heifers would.

Wasn't asking Khem (not yet two, and handicapped besides) to handle all that with no help apart from nine-year-old Heather on her pony Pablo, rather like Moses asking the sea to roll back? Of course Clarence would be ahead in the truck. But what could he do if we had trouble behind?

Pablo was good with cattle. But it was Khem's uncanny instinct for knowing which cow was going to try and dodge back, or otherwise cause trouble, and getting there to change her mind with a well-placed nip, that won the day. Khem quickly gained the herd's respect, and after that they gave up trying. It proved an uneventful cattle drive. But in concession to Khem's youth we trucked him home.

Khem loved to prance and show off. "Playing to the gallery," my Dad called it. When visitors came to see him they were never disappointed. He'd dance over to greet them on feet that seemed to float just above the ground, his tail a royal plume above the iridescent sheen of a rich liver-chestnut coat, his mane a flaming banner. After extending his dainty muzzle for a friendly pat or two, he'd whirl away to cavort on airy hooves.

If given a gunny sack he would pretend it was a mountain lion or some other such mortal enemy. People gaped as they watched him toss it high into the air, rearing to strike it as it fell, then jumping on it when it landed, stamping to pulverize this imaginary foe and grind it into the dust before reaching for it again, tearing at it with his teeth as if searching for its jugular. Then he'd fling it up into the air and the game would begin again.

Such was Khem's charisma, his quality, and his charm that most people were too caught up in the whole to be repelled by the unsightly, gaping hollow that should have housed the second window of his soul.

Apart from being a disfiguring blemish, Khem's blindness never seriously affected him as a saddle horse. Nor did he, in all the years I had him, ever misjudge and step on my toes or brush against me. He seemed so finely tuned he could sense exactly where I stood and so avoid bumping me. It was uncanny.

Why can't the two-eyed horses of this world who seem to take delight in tramping on feet not their own have a shot or two of his solicitude?

Khem and I logged a lot of miles together. It might be finding a runaway heifer that had escaped and gone across the river, cutting her out of her adopted herd, changing her mind about not wanting to cross a bridge, and finally getting her hazed back to our Rocky Ridges Ranch corrals ... in itself a day's work for most horses. But Khem still had fourteen miles to go. I could arrive home feeling tired and almost beat, but the bounce in Khem's step, the fire in his eye, the gay

arch to his tail said he could be coming out of his corral after a two-day rest. Looking at him made my own
weariness drop away.

Khem and his owner, Mary Burpee ready for their morning ride.

However, once Khem and I took on a cattle job we
didn't quite finish. That time giving up was my idea,
not his.

We went to drive a neighbour's cow out of one of
our hay fields, which should have been a simple ten-
minute job. But this cow, like other ornery bovines, had
her own ideas about were she was going ... or not going
... so Khem figured a little nip would change her mind.
Normally it does. This time the cow dropped in her
tracks as if someone had put a bullet in her brain. Khem
looked surprised, then reached down to nip her rump
again. He'd find out if she was alive or not.

The cow bellowed, threw a wild look back at us, and
didn't move. Khem was willing to paw her into some

sort of activity but I was worried she might have had a heart attack, or some form of paralysis. Maybe a nerve got pinched by his nip. Even though it had only been a very small nip. She had certainly looked normal enough before flopping down. In fact she looked normal enough now, except she wouldn't, or couldn't, get up. I rode home to phone the neighbour.

It wasn't long until I saw Art and his girlfriend Ruby drive into the field in their pick-up truck. They appeared to be having a spot of trouble with the critter, so after putting dinner in the oven I rode back down to help. The cow (she had been up) was down again and Art was prodding her with an old abandoned fence-post.

Just as I got close enough to call out "Is she paralyzed?" she lurched to her feet, bellowing like an enraged water buffalo, and charged Art. Quick as a flash Khem ducked in and nipped her on the shoulder. The cow changed course and came after us. No problem, I thought. Just keep ahead of her and maybe we can lure her out the gate. It didn't work.

Realizing there was no hope of catching Khem, she whirled and went for Art again. This time he clobbered her with a stick and she dropped like a rock.

"Whew! What do we do now?" I had never seen an animal like this before.

Art gave a sickly grin. "I'll get the ... (and being an old army sergeant he wasn't one to stint on descriptive expletives) ... up. If she turns on you try to get the ... (more colourful words) ... to follow you out the gate. Once she's on the road Ruby and I won't have any trouble getting her home."

I wasn't so sure. To me that gleam in her eye spelled trouble.

Art swung his stick. The cow lurched to her feet with the grace of a mating walrus and was after him at a heavy pounding gallop. As before, Khem ducked in to nip her shoulder. She churned out a long, complaining bellow and went for the stallion. He danced away, daring her to catch him. She accepted the challenge but soon turned her attention back to the man again. Chasing Art took less effort.

Hoping to draw her away from Art, Khem whirled and bit her on the rump. She went down like a drunk falling off a roof.

I was sure there had to be something wrong with the animal. This wasn't normal cow behaviour. But Art said, "Na. The cantankerous old son-of-a-bitch does this all the time. It's because she's ornery ... doesn't like being driven."

"If I went for a pail of oats would she follow you?" I sounded hopeful.

Art shot me a look that said I must be out of my mind. "You keep luring her towards the gate, like you've been doing. Soon as we have her out onto the road she'll head home without any more trouble."

I hoped so, for this sort of thing wasn't to my liking. I kept getting this niggling feeling there must be something about Khem or about me that was upsetting her. Maybe if we weren't here ... ? But Art didn't think so. And she was his cow. So what the heck. We carried on.

I don't know how many times the cow went down ... how many times she lunged after Art ... how many times she turned to charge Khem, before we finally got her out the gate and heading down the road towards her own pasture. It seemed to take a long time.

Art pushed back his sweat-stained hat and brushed away the droplets of water standing on his forehead.

"Thanks for the help, Mary. She'll go okay now. Ruby and I'll follow her in the truck."

"Well, okay, if you're sure you can manage." I still wondered if it might be some quirky aversion to horses causing her abnormal behaviour. Anyway, I'd left dinner in the oven. Clarence would be coming in from the field and wondering what had happened to me. I'd better get home. "If she gives you any more trouble let me know and I'll come and help again." The words drifted back on the wind as Khem lit out for home like a too-long confined rocket.

Two days later I heard what happened after I left. Or at least I heard Art's version.

It seems the cow had given no trouble at first, but after a while she decided to turn and head back. For such a big lanky critter with hide stretched tight as a drum-head across her raw-boned hips, she could move with amazing agility when she wanted to. Both Art and Ruby jumped out of the truck, waving their sticks in an attempt to turn her.

When Art clouted her she went down again. But this time when she got up, with Khem not there to distract her, she went for Ruby.

Now Ruby is a solid chunk of a woman of generous proportions, and she wasn't about to back away from any cow. She had helped her Dad far too often as he went about the countryside doctoring sick animals to be afraid of them.

But perhaps this once she should have been like Irish Pat, who claimed "Bejabers an 'tisn't better to be a coward for five minutes than a dead man all me life?"

According to Art, the cow rammed Ruby and tossed her ten feet into the air.

"Ten feet? You've got to be kidding."

"Nope. That's right." Art looked vaguely offended.

"And after that?"

"Dad-blamed critter walked the rest of the way home just as peaceful as you please. She knew all the time where she was supposed to go."

"You'll load her out on the next cattle truck of course?" I couldn't imagine keeping an animal like that around.

"Naw. She raises good calves. She'll be okay s'long as she don't stray away from the herd. Then she'll get to actin' owly agin."

Ruby, apart from feeling as if she had been attacked by a bulldozer, wasn't seriously hurt

I couldn't help wondering if Art's stories (he's an avid fisherman) might grow with the telling. But Rudy didn't deny it.

Anyway, that was the one time Khem and I started something we didn't really finish.

When Khem saw me lugging his saddle and bridle into the corral he'd streak towards me like an untamed whirlwind, head up, ears pricked, mane and tail flying. Anyone not knowing him would have turned and raced for the safety of the fence. I knew he'd slam to a stop inches from me, reach for the bit, then wait for the bridle to be fastened and the saddle put on and cinched. He enjoyed our daily rides as much as I did.

Khem and I began entering area parades decked out in Arabian costume. The public and the judges seemed so taken with his charisma and magnetic appearance they overlooked the gaping hole disfiguring his face.

He garnered a lot of red ribbons.

This was when his brother Ramose, in Calgary, was taking Alberta show circles in his stride. Yet I was hearing that many people, including those at the Bear Claw Ranch who had bred both of them, considered Khem the better horse.

Maybe, just maybe, Khem could do well at halter despite his disfigurement and my ignorance about show ring procedure. We decided to give it a try, choosing the Vermilion Horse Show for our debut.

Today's show people would shudder at the way I led him into the ring in the same western bridle he wore when chasing cows back on the ranch. Although whips in the show ring were not as prevalent then as they were to become, the other stallion handlers in the class carried them. I carried nothing. If I had, Khem would have thought it was something to play with.

I know now I turned the wrong way when presenting Khem to the judge, and I didn't stand him up in the accepted manner. But despite all my faults Khem won first ribbon. Afterwards the judge (a man reputed to have forgotten more about horses than most judges ever knew) asked me to stand Khem parallel to the grandstands so people could see how a true classical Arabian should look. My hat suddenly felt too tight.

Khem won several stallion classes at Vermilion (the only place we ever showed him) before we decided to go whole hog by entering him at Edmonton's prestigious Aurora Arabian show where professional trainers would parade "the best in the West" before the judge.

This time Clarence would go with me because if we went up the afternoon before Khem's morning class and came home immediately afterwards we wouldn't lose much haying time.

As Khem stepped into the back of our truck the dust went reeling across the yard in stinging little pellets. The milk cow, bullied by the wind, watched us with her back hunched against the gale, her tail cowed between her legs. Surely it was only a local squall and we would soon drive out of it.

We didn't. It got worse.

The wind howled and gusted for the entire three-hour trip, whipping up a black blizzard that pelted the truck and flew between the openings in the stock-racks to bombard the horse with the stinging persistence of sand missiles. The straw at his feet was lifted to swirl around in an explosive maelstrom that got in his eyes and up his nostrils and irritated his sensitive hide.

The air, thick and churning with dust and dirt and straw, was a torment that clung to Khem like a leech, sucking at his patience. For the first and only time in his life, he kicked at the truck end-gate.

When finally the city skyline loomed dark and jagged through the dust clouds, like mountains on the western horizon, I let out my breathe with a swoosh of relief. Soon now Khem would be stabled, and out of this horrible wind.

The iridescent sheen that normally made his dark coat shine so brilliantly people would remark "I can almost see myself in him" had been replaced by a dull film of dirt. His mane and tail were snarled in straw. His face was filthy, his nostrils layered in congealed dust, the cavity of his blind eye looked like a muddy ravine, and his good eye was watering, its tears weaving a murky trail through the dust on the crooked white stripe that was his special insignia. I felt sick.

Later that evening, after much grooming, Khem looked almost normal again except for his good eye. And no matter how many times I bathed that, it persisted in watering. I knew it was sore.

Khem spent a restless night. I heard every move, and

suffered with him. Damn! What if Khem lost his good eye? All because I had dragged him up here, selfishly wanting the prestige of having a famous stallion.

By morning the eye was still watering but not so badly, so we got ready for his class, hoping that it might pass unnoticed.

As I led Khem among the other stallions in the holding area all eyes were on him, for no one could fail to notice so regal a horse, his shimmering liver-chestnut coat a vivid contrast to the red of proudly crested mane and arched tail. Among this group of champions he was the horse that stood out.

I had never shown in an indoor arena before and for some strange reason Khem and I were first in the line-up of horses being presented to the judge.

Other stallions were close behind. Maybe Khem was still upset from the truck trip yesterday, or maybe he merely objected to having a strange stallion come too close on his blind side. But whatever the reason he kicked at the horse next him as a warning for him to keep his distance. He didn't hit anything so no harm was done ... unless it was to give the judge a bad view of his manners.

When the judge was making his placings Khem didn't merit a second look. I could have crawled in a hole, until he called me over after the winners had left the ring to say Khem had the best body he had ever seen on an Arabian. If only he had made that announcement publicly Khem's honour would have been upheld.

I was learning that politics and patronage rear their ugly heads even at horse shows.

Shortly after that I asked a woman who was recognized as one of Canada's top Arabian judges how she would place a one-eyed stallion in a halter class (which I saw as a breeding class where superficial disfigurements shouldn't be taken into account), provided he was as good as, or better than, others in the line-up.

Her answer floored me and spelled finish to any desire to ever show Khem again. "I would never place a one-eyed horse." Her voice, crackling with authority, had come marching in from high places on decisive tread.

So Khem's accident not only cost him an eye; it cost the entire Arabian breed.

Under a different set of circumstances Khem's contribution to the breed could have equalled that of any of the great stallions of his time. Had he been unblemished and shown as most other Arabian stallions were, he would surely have won the recognition he deserved, and more breeders would have made use of his services. Instead, only a limited number of horsemen who chanced to see him realized his potential for improving the breed.

One day a grizzled old rancher from south of the Neutral Hills, his face lean and hard and wrinkled by years of sun, wind and saddle, sat beside me on the top rail of our corral, squinting knowingly at Khem from under the shaded brim of his sweat-stained hat.

I had been telling him how I had been cutting out wayward steers that morning from a neighbour's herd where the pasture was a nightmare of buck brush and silver willow hiding badger holes, pocket-gopher mounds, and sand blow-outs. Not the terrain one would choose for a neck or nothing ride, or a cutting competition.

"Dag-nab it, woman! With legs like those, if that horse put his foot in a badger hole he'd pull it out and keep right on going and you'd never know it. Best bone and tendons I've ever seen...." His voice drifted off, almost as if he was talking to himself. Year later Bazy Tankersley, owner of America's prestigious Al Marah's Arabian stud farm, made the same remark after she had seen a picture of Khem as an aged stallion.

In all the years I rode Khem he only went down with me twice. The first time he was flying down the road at a ground-covering gait that was neither trot nor gallop but is what in some breeds is called a rack. It was rocking-chair smooth and so fast ordinary horses had to break into a lively gallop to keep up.

This day a pocket-gopher had undermined the road, without making a mark on the surface. While the covering of gravel looked normal enough, it was in effect an invitation to disaster. Khem, perhaps because the road surface was smooth and hard and he wasn't prepared for anything else, went down when his foot broke through the surface into the run below, but he made such a gallant effort to regain his feet I scarcely touched ground before he was up again.

The next time he fell it was different. It was late October. A light covering of snow, the first of the season, had fallen in the night. Not enough to make dirt roads or grass ditches slippery. So there seemed no reason to expect trouble in moving the cattle herd, which had been brought up the day before for warble-fly treatment, back across the highway.

What I hadn't realized was that highway traffic had turned the snow on the pavement into black ice. So when Khem and I headed onto it and he had to turn quickly to stop a cow from cutting back, his feet shot out from under him and he went down hard, crushing my ankle beneath him. He scrambled up, but I couldn't walk. I had to cling to his mane and let him half drag me out of the line of traffic. Then I slumped to the side of the road to wait for Clarence to finish putting the cows through the pasture gate and get back to me. He hadn't realized what had happened.

The result of that fall was torn ligaments and a sprained ankle that kept me on crutches for weeks. I was still hobbling in March.

Normally I rode all winter ... except when it was blizzarding or the mercury was cowering into a frozen blob. That winter I didn't ride at all; I scarcely even went out. So Khem spent his days walking the paddock fence, watching the house. Clarence said he whinnied every time I stepped outside, even if it was only to shake a mat, or feed the dog.

In mid-March I couldn't stand being house-bound another moment. I had to get out into the spring sunshine, find out if I could still ride, because it would soon be time for the annual spring cattle drive and I didn't want to miss it. Khem danced impatiently as I swung the saddle onto his back and cinched it. When I opened the corral gate and led him out he was exploding with excitement.

I must be crazy to think I could ride such a bundle of dynamite. A horse that hadn't been ridden, hadn't been longed, hadn't even been out of his paddock since October, and was in a rush now to make up for all those lost months and lost gallops.

My ankle was still very weak. I walked with extreme care. Just to step on the tiniest pebble had me grimacing with pain. I'd never be able to handle Khem. I'd better get someone else to ride him eight or ten miles to get the edge off. Maybe after that I could manage him.

But what the heck! He was *my* horse. I didn't *want* anyone else riding him.

Khem's feet danced with poorly suppressed anticipation as I got one foot in the stirrup and hauled myself up, trying to ignore the pain that shot up my leg, and settled quickly into the saddle. I had to be ready ... ready for I didn't quite know what.

Instead of floating away in a wild, glad gallop Khem didn't move. A change had come over him. He stopped fidgeting and looked back, sensing something wasn't right. When he did move it was at a walk, sedate and cadenced.

Never once during that ride did he attempt to go faster than a walk. The gallop I knew he had been longing for was put on hold. Even a prairie chicken whirring up out of the snow right under his nose didn't bring the startled leap it normally would have done. I felt his muscles tense momentarily, then relax as if he had reminded himself, "Be careful. Your rider isn't herself today."

Riding proved to be good therapy for my ankle. It began to show marked improvement after every ride, but until it was better Khem stayed solicitous of my safety.

I often rode Khem alongside other stallions, geldings, mares, even mares in heat, and he was always well-behaved and easily managed. Always the perfect gentleman. So I had no concerns the day I agreed to go riding with a group made up of school kids and adults of various ages and riding skills. There was just as much variety in their mounts.

One of Rod's school friends was riding a Shetland, a pinto gelding of no great merit. But as soon as Khem saw it he became as uptight as an over-taut fiddle string. It didn't matter if the pinto was well out in front or far to the rear, Khem seemed to be constantly watching it, waiting for a chance to attack it. Nothing like this had

ever happened before. I knew the pinto had been a fre-
quent visitor to our farm, but what sort of exchange
could there have been between the two to cause my normally well-behaved stallion to be showing such a violent
hatred of a Shetland gelding? Rod's friend was warned to
never again tie his Shetland anywhere near Khem's paddock. Not even where the stallion could see him.

In a breed known for its intelligence, gentleness and
people-loving disposition, Khem was outstanding—
and he passed these qualities on to his get—but he was-
n't perfect. He'd have killed that pony if he got a chance,
just as he killed a couple of calves that were foolish
enough to squeeze into his paddock. Khem went for
them with his teeth, broke their backs, then trampled
them. Yet the few times he got out with the cattle in
their area, he didn't hurt them. He totally ignored
them. It was as if he knew he was the interloper. So perhaps when he killed calves he was only defending his
territory.

Or perhaps he was remembering the tragedy of his
eye. It was a tragedy that would claim his life.

When Khem was twenty-four people seeing him for
the first time took him for a twelve-year-old. Clarence
and I, on the other hand, were growing increasingly
worried about him. The cavity that had once housed an
eye looked red and sore. It oozed matter ... and that
matter developed a foul smell. We were prepared to have
him put down, but the veterinarians said, "No. Not yet.
He's too good a horse. Let's try an operation. If it's successful he could live for years."

The operation found what we had expected. A can-
cerous tumour. But the Vets didn't tell us the dread disease had already spread to the bone. So we lived for a
while under a false blanket of hope.

In Horse Hospital Khem won the hearts of those who worked with him. An assistant Vet took Khem for a walk every day in the park and folks seeing him would stop to watch. And admire. It was hard to believe such a magnificent-looking horse didn't have a long life stretching ahead of him.

At first we believed the operation had "got it all." Then horrible reality raised its grisly head. Cancer, nagging, debilitating cancer from which there is no escape, had Khem firmly in its clutches. Yet he stayed light of step and proud of heart. Disease might waste away his flesh, but never his spirit.

There were those even in the last month who said of Khem, "Vets make mistakes. That horse doesn't have cancer. He looks too good." But those of us who knew him best and loved him most knew he was failing.

He was too noble a horse, too faithful a friend. We couldn't let him suffer. He must not be allowed to die by inches.

On June 14, 1982 (the day before his actual twenty-sixth birthday), the Vet was to come at 1 p.m. and send Khem on his last long journey. Relief from pain seemed the kindest birthday present we could give a horse who had been my friend and companion for so many years.

Khem had serviced two or three mares that spring but none had settled, which in itself told us the cancer was worsening its hold. However, the morning of the 14th (the day the Vet was to come) Gango Fantasy, my favourite mare, was in season, and more to give Khem one final pleasure than from any hope of a foal, we let him breed her. When he dismounted the feeling persisted that he had been determined to leave me one last gift. A part of himself.

(Eleven months later that gift arrived. An exquisite little filly.)

I felt like a Judas when I arranged for the Vet to come and put Khem to sleep, yet I had to do it. I couldn't let him die by inches, but I couldn't bear to see it happen. Clarence, who loved him too, would be with him.

The numbing sense of loss was closing in on me, compressing my mind like steel bands. I knew I was seeing Khem for the last time. A sob choked my throat as I watched him float across the corral towards me for one last pat, heard him whinny as I left the yard.

I was conditioning Gango Eldorado, his gelding son, for a 200-mile trek that was coming up soon, but today Eldorado chose his own trails, his own gait. I was too teary-eyed and blubbery to see, too upset to care where we went. It hadn't been easy to sign the death warrant of a horse who had been my special friend and faithful companion for so many years.... I felt shattered, totally devastated.

I was gone a long time before I finally turned and rode slowly homewards. By now Clarence would have Khem buried out where we had so often ridden. That seemed to give me some small comfort.

As ranchers I was not unfamiliar with the sight of a dead animal, but I didn't want to see Khem's body. Without the fire, the spirit, the charisma, and all those special somethings that were uniquely Khem, it would have looked like so much clay.

The yard seemed unnaturally quiet. No sign of Clarence. Or his vehicle. Resolutely I kept my eyes from wandering towards the corral that had been Khem's.

Suddenly there was a sound that jerked the hairs along my spine to soldier-stiff attention. Don't be stupid. That whinny wasn't Khem's. How could it be?

Khem was dead. My imagination was making some other horse sound like him.

Then it came again. My eyes swept past the barn and I was hit with staggering reality. Khem was alive. He was up there looking at me, welcoming me home as he had always done. My mind reeled. The full portent of what I was seeing smashed into me with the force of a killer hurricane.

Questions whirled through my head. What had happened? The Vet should have come and gone hours ago. And where was Clarence? Why wasn't he around? I hurried the gelding into the barn, patted Khem almost as if there was a need to convince myself he was real, and then raced to the house. Something must be wrong.

On the table was a note from Clarence. "Trouble at the Veterinary Clinic. The Vet can't make it before five." It was already 4:45. I gave an involuntary shiver, stricken with the futility of it all.

I was tempted to take the car and leave. Clarence had said he would be back.

But what the heck! Hadn't I been with Khem, shared the other crises in his life? Hadn't we always seen them through together? Now in this his last and final crises how could I have ever thought of deserting him … to let him face it on his own? Damn it! What sort of a coward was I?

Numbly I stuffed my pockets full of horse crunchies, took Khem's halter off its peg, and went into the corral. Clarence came, considerate as always, asking if I didn't want to go. But I said, "No. Khem and I have been through too much together. I'm not going to let him face death without me at his side. I'll lead him out. He knows me best."

As the Vet was readying the needle I tried to feed

Khem the crunchies that where his special treat. But for the first time in his life he didn't want them.

I had hoped he wouldn't know what we were doing to him. But he knew.

The needle found his jugular. His proud tail lowered, the light left his eye, his head drooped, he staggered and fell. I dropped the rope and walked away, not seeing or caring where I went.

Khem was now with the other gods on Mount Olympus.

Chapter Twelve

Khem's Kids and Mine

It had begun like any ordinary summer morning. No hint that tragedy was skulking behind the long ribbons of sunshine festooning the landscape, flecking it alternately into patchworks of sparkling promise and sombre shadows.

Then the tranquility of my day was shattered. Heather, gasping for breath, her mouth quivering as if uncertain whether she ought to laugh or cry, burst through the door. Her eyes were like small moons, her voice vacillating between jubilation and total disaster. "Shasta has a foal. Except it won't move."

My brain did an instant flip-flop. I grabbed a hat and headed out the door. It was too soon. The mare wasn't due for another six weeks, yet a tiny thread of hope persisted until I saw the body. The perfectly formed replica of Shasta had never moved. And it never would. I had to pull away the amniotic sac encasing its hindquarters to know it was a colt.

Chilling numbness filled the pit of my stomach. Our first Arabian foal, dead. Only weeks after Khem's tragic accident had left him disfigured for life. Suddenly the land seemed to have become tense under a sky that had taken on a hard metallic glare, a glare that gave every blade of grass, every tiny shadow an aura of gloom. Even the air seemed dark and oppressive. Was this a portent of things to come?

I led Shasta home at a funeral pace. The hammering in my mind was unable to block out the frightening squish of a placenta that flopped and writhed like something alive as it wrapped and unwrapped itself from around the mare's back legs at every step.

Clarence, outside the shop changing cultivator shovels, dropped his tools and stood up. His sweeping glance saw not just Shasta but the glaze of shock clouding my eyes. His long legs ate up the distance between us with a sort of compassionate urgency. He opened his arms and with a shuddering sob I moved into them, as if somehow his closeness would bring a miracle.

Heather patted my arm, her small hand trying to bring comfort. "Please don't cry, Mummy. God likes little colts too."

Clarence held me quietly for a few minutes, then handed me a Kleenex tissue. I dredged up a sodden sigh and pulled out of the comforting circle of his arms. It was time to get back to cold reality. Shasta hadn't cleaned. Bloody strands of afterbirth slapped her back legs in a gory-tentacled embrace each time she moved.

Clarence's voice sounded strained. "Mares are more vulnerable to infection from retained placenta than cows. If Shasta's isn't taken away quickly she may founder and never be able to conceive again." That bit of information didn't do much to drag my spirits up out of the dust.

It was a worried, hurried trip to the Vet Clinic. Maybe raising horses hadn't been such a great idea.

When we got back home again with Shasta it was time to face the cold reality of the situation. Our plans to raise Arabians had met with devastating setbacks. There was no denying that. But we couldn't, we wouldn't let ourselves think they were omens of things to come.

A year later Shasta, this time carrying Khem's foal, was nearing parturition. With the fetus almost full term there seemed no reason to expect a repetition of last year.

Neither Shasta nor Gyp, a black thoroughbred mare already two weeks overdue, had waxed up yet. Horsemen who knew much more about horses than I did all claimed, "When you see wax on a mare's tits you can count on her foaling within 12 to 36 hours." I still believed the experts.

The morning sang of summer. Both mares were grazing in a small pasture near the barn. No wax on their tits. Foaling seemed the last thing on either of their minds, so I offered to go to Wainwright to pick up a belt for the drill-fill. It would save Clarence from having to shut down seeding to go for it.

When I got back with the belt I expected my husband to be in for dinner, but there was no sign of him. Or the mares. I hurried out to make a quick check. If either mare was waxing up I needed to know.

Then I saw Clarence. And immediately knew something was wrong. The droop of his shoulders whirled my mind back to the time ten of our cows had broken through the ice and drowned. He must have had a serious break-down.

Was it the tractor? The seed drill? Or ... ?

"What's wrong?" I called, wondering if it would mean another hurried trip for repairs.

His voice sounded as if his words were being grated over a rusty hoof rasp. "Shasta's had her foal. It was through the fence."

I felt as if I'd just been bashed over the head with a plank. "Were you able to get it back?"

"Yes." His tone was so uncharacteristically flat and non-committal I asked the next question with difficulty.

"Is it ... is it all right?"

"No."

Shasta had foaled too close to a fence and the filly,

for it was a filly, had either been pushed under the bottom wire in the birthing process or had flopped under it in her first struggles to stand. In trying to get back to her mother she got a mass of jagged cuts crisscrossing her chest and front legs. They might not leave permanent scars, but they would need daily care.

Apart from that the filly seemed healthy ... healthier than Shasta, who for the second time in her life hadn't cleaned. She was in such a dither, so uptight, she wouldn't stand to let the foal nurse. Our normally calm mare was behaving worse than a wild Highland heifer.

"Mary, talk to her, try to calm her down; keep her still long enough for me to get the foal to where it can nurse." The brusqueness in Clarence's voice said he might be quickly losing his patience.

I crooned soothing nothings into Shasta's ear, massaged her withers with one hand, gave her halter sharp twitches with the other whenever she threatened to kick the foal Clarence was manoeuvring, with some difficulty, into lunch-position. Finally a wave of relief flowed over me.

The wet smacking sounds said the filly's lips had found a tit and closed on it hungrily. The moment it began suckling Shasta's maternal instincts re-surfaced. From then on she was an ideal mother. But her problems with retained placenta persisted.

A trip to the veterinarian would take care of the mechanics of removing it, but I had to learn to insert uterine boluses into the uterus of a mare. Fortunately Shasta was gentle and had no objection to me shoving my arm into her warm, moist private parts. By pushing it in clear up to the armpit I was just able to reach the horns of her uterus where the boluses were supposed to go.

But she did object to Clarence giving her hypodermic needles. The moment he walked into the barn she'd break out in a sweat and start to fidget and dance. Her muscles would tense up until they were as hard as old pemmican.

A succession of broken needles, spilled penicillin, testy tempers, and frayed nerves made me decide it was time to get over being squeamish about giving needles. I'd give the penicillin to Shasta myself. She was accustomed to having me handling her. She wouldn't be suspecting the worst the moment I walked in beside her.

When she was relaxed and not uptight the jab of a needle was no worse than the bite of a troublesome fly.

The previous year the veterinarians had assured us, "Retained placenta is rare in mares. It's not likely to ever happen again."

But it had. And it would again, and again. It became a recurring problem that we had to learn to live with. It happened for fourteen of Shasta's seventeen deliveries. The veterinarians had no explanations for it except "Her miscarriage must have caused scarring of the uterus."

Any ordinary mare with this problem would have found herself going down the road, but Shasta was no ordinary mare. She was a great producer, and a great baby-sitter. It was common to see a dainty foal frisking beside her, two little girls on her back, and a small boy following, hoping for a chance to climb on too. I never worried about my youngsters when they rode Shasta. She took the same good care of them as she did her own.

Sha-Em, the filly Clarence had found through the fence, was only a day old when we began getting concerned about her. The wire cuts must be a lot worse than they looked. The wee animal seemed unnaturally listless. She looked as droopy as lettuce leaves in a prolonged drought, yet she appeared to be nursing. The cuts weren't festering. What could be wrong? She repeatedly acted as if she was about to lie down, then changed her mind.

Clarence, squinting against the hot glare of the sun, his thumbs hooked into the braces of his overalls, watched with a thoughtful expression on his well-tanned face. "Have you ever seen her lying down?" I shook my head. Heather and Terry Lee shook theirs too.

"I think what that filly needs is sleep. When she starts to lie down her cuts hurt more. If she stands still they don't feel so bad. So she's got it figured out that lying down is wrong for her. Foals can't sleep standing up, not like older horses." A frown fingered across Clarence's forehead as he reached for the filly, gathered her in his arms and laid her gently on the ground.

The tiny animal promptly began threshing and flailing in a wild attempt to regain her feet. Her primordial instincts were "Jump up. Run. Escape."

Clarence leaned across the little bundle of dynamite, holding her down with his own body until she gave a ragged sigh and relaxed. Then Heather whispered, "Can I hold her now, Daddy?"

At his nod she eased herself down beside the filly. Cradling the exquisite little head on her lap she stroked the slender neck, brushing away flies and mosquitoes, crooning reassurance every time a contented sigh shivered through the filly. Sha-Em slept.

For the next two hours, if the dogs barked, or four-year-old Rod dared to shout, or someone let the screen door bang, Terry Lee turned on them like an avenging angel, hissing, "Keep quiet! Sha-Em's sleeping."

That afternoon a bonding took place between Heather and the filly that was to last a lifetime.

"Mom, can I do that?" Now Heather wanted to be the one to bathe and dress Sha-Em's cuts. Evenings would find her in the walkway behind Shasta's stall, straddling a milking stool, a basin of disinfectant beside her and Sha-Em facing her. The filly might be experimentally nuzzling the 10-year-old's hair, sniffing at the basin, or standing fascinated as she watched what was going on beyond the open door. Always the halter shank dangled loose on the ground.

Washing the day's accumulation of dirt from the cuts and smearing on ointment hurt, no matter how gently Heather worked. Yet the filly, as if understanding this hurt was done from love, never attempted to move away. She could have ... she was never tied.

One evening an out-of-district rancher watched the pair in wide-eyed disbelief, then exclaimed, "I could work with my foals a million years and they'd never be that quiet." The next day he brought two mares to Khem.

As the weeks progressed we knew Sha-Em had to be Heather's. There was a special bond between them that was too precious to lose.

Sha-Em was barely eighteen months old when Heather rode her for the very first time. She used a rubber-bitted bridle, but no saddle. The filly was behaving well, stopping and starting on command, quietly circling the corral or walking through figure-eight patterns for Heather.

Then, as unexpectedly as if he had been dropped from above, a big billy goat came stalking around the corner of the barn, looking as if he owned the place and was prepared to fight for it. His smell was strong enough to kill a skunk a hundred yards upwind.

Chickens ran squawking for the safety of their hen house, cows bellowed and grouped together, uncertain whether they ought to charge the intruder or make a dash for the pasture.

Sha-Em had never seen (or smelled) a billy goat before. Her eyes bugged out, her nostrils flared; she whirled to run.

"When she did I was scared. I didn't know what might happen," Heather told us later. "But when I pulled up on the lines and said 'whoa' she stopped. She was shaking with fright but I talked to her and she didn't try to run again."

Years later I watched a small boy get boosted up onto one of Sha-Em's brothers and ride him into a paddock where adult riders were exercising horses (stallions, mares, and geldings) in readiness for a jumping class. The lad's father, looking smart and confident in English riding togs, said in a voice that rang with pride, "That stallion's disposition alone is worth a million dollars."

Remarks like this were not unfamiliar to us. We had come to take great dispositions for granted in our Arabs. Other folks, owning Khem's get for the first time, were in for a pleasant surprise.

The year Sha-Em was a two-year-old Heather began pestering us about riding her in the Hardisty Stampede parade. Not riding her in ordinary western gear, but in an Arabian costume flowing with glitz and glamour.

Our daughter was no stranger to parades. She had ridden in her first as an Indian maiden before she was five. It was a parade to celebrate one of Hughenden's milestones, but my mother was convinced I'd taken leave of my senses when she heard Heather would be riding in it. "Mary, surely you and Clarence don't intend to let Heather ride Nifty? Why, he's scarcely more than a colt." Her tone was brittle, her face taut with worry.

"Don't worry Mom. I'll be riding right beside her on Pompey, and I'll have Nifty's lead rope, so she'll be *okay*." But my mother worried anyway … so much that she couldn't bring herself to come out and watch the parade.

A few years later Heather, in another Indian costume, had ridden Pablo, a Shetland stallion, in Hardisty's rodeo parade. Another time she and Terry Lee in Mexican sombreros and capes had ridden Peter and Cottontail, two Mexican burros, in the Hardisty parade. Tagging beside them was Cottontail's two-week-old daughter, Perky, carrying a tiny blanket and a teddy-bear wearing a sombrero. Perky stole the show … until she bucked and the teddy-bear hit the dust.

Heather ready to ride the Shetland stallion Pablo in the Hardisty rodeo parade.

Peter and Cottontail didn't behave too well that day either.

About half-way through the parade they suddenly streaked off towards the river. Finally, when the burros decided they had gone far enough, the girls were able to get them turned around and back in time to join up with the tail-end of the parade. Peter's popularity hit zero that day with Heather.

She refused him even one bite of her ice cream cone ... though he pleaded for it with a hard-to-resist look in his mournful eyes and a bray so shrill it startled people two blocks away.

When Terry Lee offered him the wrapper off her chocolate bar he ate it with a soulful look that said here was a donkey without a friend in the world. Her heart melted. "I think he really is sorry for being so bad, Heather. Here, Peter, I'll share my candy bar."

But ponies and Mexican burros were definitely not a young, spirited Arabian. So this time I said "No" in a way that slammed the door on any further arguing.

The silk cape, the flowing robes, the dangling tassels on the caparison would all be waiting to catch every vagrant breeze that came their way. If they weren't enough to spook a young horse, there would be floats ablaze with glitter, crackling with pulsating plastics and fluttering balloons, some of which were sure to pop at the most inopportune time. There would be marching bands, half-wild buffalo, covered wagons, painted clowns, creaking machinery, long-horned steers ... one never knew what weird entries would show up.

Sha-Em had never been off the ranch; she wasn't mature enough to handle so much excitement. "Maybe next year, Heather. When you're both older."

Heather looked slightly miffed as she went out the

door but she didn't hang around to press her case. That surprised me a little, for she was an Eve not easily talked out of her apple.

I saw both girls ride bareback down to the hay field, Terry Lee on her black-and-white pony Butterfly, and Heather on Sha-Em, and thought nothing of it. Their Dad was down there mowing.

I had just put a chocolate cake in the oven and finished crimping the edges of an apple pie for supper when Terry Lee, her face glowing like an young angel who has just been handed her first harp, stuck her head inside the screen door. "Mom! Come quick! Heather wants you to look at Sha-Em!"

Good grief! What now? A flashback of another time gripped my brain. The winter four-year-old Heather had come bursting through the door, her voice shrill with excitement and the importance of her message. "Guess what, Mom? A whole bunch of our cows, ten of them, broke through the ice on the dug-out at Rocky Ridges and they all drowned. Except for one that was one still alive when we got there. As soon as Daddy got her pulled out of the water I helped him rub her all over with straw to try and dry her off. Then we covered her up with more straw and lit fires around her, hoping to warm her up." Heather had stopped to catch her breath before adding matter-of-factly, "But she'll probably die. Her legs were so cold and stiff they stuck straight out ... like wooden fence posts."

I quickly pushed that memory aside. It was one of those things best forgotten (but the cow had lived).

This time Heather's grin, when I opened the screen door and stepped outside, gave her face an elfish look that suggested she might have just made a good deal with the "wee people" and wanted the world to know it. But what of Sha-Em? She was so loaded down with bulging gunny-sacks she was like one of the heavily laden burros one sees in foreign lands. Only her head, tail and legs were showing. There were wisps of sweet-smelling hay protruding from well-filled jute bags balanced across her withers, hanging on either side and over her rump.... And Heather sat proudly among them like a queen on her throne, her face glowing with a "Now what're you going to say Mom?" smile.

"See how sensible Sha-Em is, Mom. These bags don't scare her. So why can't I ride her in the parade? Please, Mom." The pleading look in her eyes was almost as hard to resist as her logic.

"How did you get the bags up onto her back" I demanded without bothering to answer her.

"Easy. After we filled the bags I got back on Sha-Em, and Terry Lee shoved the sacks one at a time up onto Butterfly's back. Then I just had to reach down and pull them up onto Sha-Em. It worked real good."

"You girls did it by yourselves? With no help from your father?" My voice sounded definitely suspicious.

"Of course not, Mom. Dad's busy haying." The tone implied I'd asked a stupid question.

Heather rode Sha-Em in the parade. And they won a ribbon.

When Terry Lee became our little show lady, Gango Firefly (Sha-Em's younger sister) was the horse important in her life.

Only a show-mother can know both the thrill of watching her child win against professionals and the disappointment of seeing her ride out with those excused before the final line-up.

I was so proud I wanted to cry, and maybe I even did a little, the day Terry Lee rode ribbonless from the ring

Terry Lee rides Firefly at a 4-H gathering near Throne, Alberta.

patting and hugging her mare's neck so ecstatically one might have assumed Firefly had just been crowned champion of the show. Yet the judge had never once looked in her direction ... or in the direction of any of the riders who weren't from his own riding academy. That didn't matter to Terry Lee. What mattered was *she* knew her horse had given a good performance.

"Mom," Terry Lee called as I left the stands to join her. "Wasn't Firefly wonderful? She did everything I asked her to do. Just perfectly. Mrs. Bonnello would be so proud of her."

Mrs. Bonnello, the lady at whose Donsdale Stables Terry Lee and Firefly had taken some dressage training, wasn't the only one proud of that pair.

I've seen Terry Lee win halter classes, and I've seen her lose them because she wouldn't compromise her principles for the sake of a ribbon. Handlers who whipped their horses to make them come charging into the ring, in the wild-eyed, nostril-flaring, almost unmanageable fashion some judges mistook for animation, had a low place in her opinion.

"Mom, Firefly is my friend. She trusts me. Isn't that more important than winning ribbons?" I agreed that it certainly was.

The man, a high-priced professional trainer, looked as if he had just been forced to drink a big dose of castor oil ... without the orange juice. He rammed his horse close to Terry Lee as she was riding Firefly from the winners' line-up carrying the trophy for Western Pleasure. It had been the first performance class at a prestigious Arabian show.

Betty, a friend sitting beside me in the stands, swore under her breath. "Good Lord! You'd think he could be more gracious with his congratulations. She's only a kid."

Betty would have swore a lot louder if she'd known what the man had really been saying.

I learned what it was from an indignant bystander who cornered me on the way to the stables.

"Mrs. Burpee, did you hear what that man was snarling at your daughter as they rode from the ring?"

I shook my head. "No. What did he say?"

"You won that class but you won't win any more. Not at this show."

When this bit of information sank in I felt stunned. There must be some mistake. No horseman would be guilty of saying such an unsportsmanlike thing. But I was wrong. The man meant every word he said. Terry Lee won no more classes at that show.

Her horse was consistently ridden into the rail. Crowded by other riders until Firefly retaliated by laying back her ears and swishing her tail. Balloons were popped low in the stands at the precise moment she cantered past, causing her to momentarily break her stride. She was harassed by front-seat catcalls and board pounding. It seemed more than a coincidence it should all happen when the judge's eyes were turned in her direction.

Yet there were other judges, at other shows, who saw ... and made allowances.

Once I overheard a judge being asked how he could justify placing Terry Lee first when her horse had so very obviously jumped and broken stride when a small dog had raced between her legs in its attempt to retrieve a tossed ball. His answer had been, "Yes, I saw that. I also saw how easily the mare came back to her rider to carry on with a perfect performance. I wouldn't have been justified in placing a pleasure class any other way."

Although there tends to be a lot of politics involved in the judging at some shows, there are judges with integrity, and a lot of courage.

It was a larger than normal 4-H horse show with many clubs taking part. Rod and his Arabian gelding, Gango Eldorado, had been the pair to beat locally. Could they do as well in these much larger classes?

I was standing ring-side watching Rod and the other contestants in a Western Pleasure class when a stranger beside me remarked, "If I was judging this class it's that chestnut Arabian right there I'd be giving the nod to. He's well put together, better hindquarters than is normally seen on Arabians these days. His rider knows what he's doing too." Secretly I agreed with him, but because I had more than a casual interest in that pair I said nothing. Nor did I tell him who I was.

In the final line-up there were suppressed gasps and raised eyebrows when a chestnut gelding whose rider was about Rod's size and build was called into first place. Obviously the judge must have seen something about Eldorado and Rod's performance he didn't like. No doubt they would be called into second place. They weren't. And not into third, fourth, fifth, or sixth place either. Well, I thought with a shrug, that's only one man's opinion.

There was a grin on Rod's face as he congratulated the winners, and as they rode chatting from the ring the judge seemed to be looking somewhat intently (I thought) at them, and then almost immediately he began thumbing through his score cards. Suddenly he beckoned to the ring steward. No doubt he wanted her to announce the next class. Instead they spent some minutes apparently in deep conversation, then the public address system was heard asking the just-excused class to return to the arena. What was going on?

When the riders and their horses were back in the ring, the judge announced he had discovered he had made a serious error. In deciding his final placings he had inadvertently missed one of the score cards and because of that it was going to change the standing of everyone in the winners' circle. He was sorry for the error, but he felt confident his action in correcting it would be in keeping with what responsible young men and women like the 4-H youth before him would have wanted. Most of those young people managed a lusty cheer when Rod and Eldorado moved to the top of the class. Not all their parents were so gracious.

I wonder how many judges would have had that man's courage.

Gango Fantasy was the result of a clandestine romance between two yearlings. She was an accident that shouldn't have happened, yet the moment she hit the ground we knew she was going to be special.

Gango Fantasy, by Image out of Wings was the result of a clandestine romance between two yearlings.

The first time Rod rode Fantasy he came back grinning as if he'd found the motherlode. "Mom. Fantasy was born green broke."

I had ridden Fantasy, now a three-year-old, only a few times when she and Eldorado made history. They may be the only Arabians in the world to have successfully herded musk oxen, but as an account of that is in the book Musk Oxen of Gango, I'll not repeat it here, except to say it was scary and it was challenging, but our horses, especially Eldorado, made us proud of them. I was proud of my son too.

With motherhood beckoning the little grey mare, it would be years before I rode Fantasy again. But she and

I had already done something few riders ... and few horses ... have even thought of attempting. We had herded musk oxen.

Chapter Thirteen

Eldorado

As a foal Eldorado looked like the last chick out of the shell.

Yet it was hard to pinpoint anything wrong with him. He had the underpinnings to win approval from thoroughbred breeders, his hindquarters were good enough to impress quarter-horse fanciers, his head and front-end were acceptable, plus he had the overall quality to bring remarks like "that animal has a lot of good breeding" from many horse enthusiasts. So what didn't I like about him? I didn't know. Whatever it was, I couldn't put my finger on it. Maybe he just lacked his father's charisma.

Eldorado was earmarked for a gelding.

This is gango Eldorado, Wing's older brother,
as he looked as a young foal.

Our son Rod, entering the magical teens and feeling he had outgrown pony days, had the chestnut picked out as his next 4-H horse. But before Eldorado became a gelding he spent time with a self-styled horseman from out of the district who was eager to breed a couple of his grade mares to him, in return for getting him well started under saddle. What a laugh that turned out to be.

When Eldorado came back to us as a gelding it seemed obvious that his training had consisted mostly of running hell-for-leather in whatever direction he was aimed. He knew nothing about neck-reining, flexing, balance, side-passing, turning on the haunches, or the forehand ... nor any of the other things a good saddle horse ought to know. Not even leads. In Eldorado's mind leads were what he did when someone snapped a rope onto his halter and said, "Come on boy." It would take Rod hours of re-training before his horse could hope to compete in 4-H competitions.

Yet right from the first there was a camaraderie between the boy and his horse. They might be racing across muddy summerfallow to outrun an escaping cow, or changing leads in the cadenced lope-through of a figure eight. It could be side-stepping to shut a gate, walking a plank teeter-totter, backing out of an ell without stepping on the flanking poles—a manoeuvre that required skill and sensitivity between horse and rider. It could be roping a calf. Or pulling on a rain slicker that was billowing like a straining sail in the breeze engendered by a galloping horse.

I learned to respect Eldorado. It would have been hard not to. He wasn't big, but what there was of him was honest ... all heart and loyalty, with horse sense and stamina thrown in for packing.

With youngsters who had never before been on a

horse, he displayed care and caution. He rarely showed the same concern for adults, especially those who fancied themselves accomplished riders. If they wanted a good gallop, by golly, they got it. Often faster ... and farther ... than they had anticipated. Eldorado loved to run and he wasn't about to stop because someone clinging to the saddle horn was frantically yelling "Stop! Stop!"

I rarely rode Eldorado, except when leading young stock to or from a pasture. I liked him for that because no matter what antics a youngster tried to pull, he never lost his cool.

Eldorado wasn't my sort of horse. Besides, why should I ride him when I had Khem? Nothing could ever really take the stallion's place, not even his elegant daughters.... Other people could admire the gelding, judge him best of the show, or point him out as "the horse with a lot of breeding" (as indeed he did have). I still saw him as the chick too late out of its shell. It wasn't until Eldorado was 17 that I began to fully appreciate him.

I should have known something unusual was on the wires the evening a Saskatchewan friend, Allen Murdoch, showed up, resplendent in a beard that had taken on magisterial proportions. He could have stepped out of the annals of history. Or flown in from the North Pole.

"Well, Murdoch, what's up with you?" Clarence grinned as I put the kettle on for tea.

Allen's eyes—they were about all you could see of his face—were all sparkle and kinetic energy. "I'm fixing up a covered wagon, prairie schooner style."

Before I could explode with "What on earth for?" he continued. "The cities of Moose Jaw and Saskatoon are celebrating their dual centenaries with a colony trek in

June. Basically we'll be following the same route, living under the same primitive conditions as those colonists who first made the trek one hundred years ago. Of course there will have to be a few concessions made to civilization. Things like camp stoves instead of open fires, portable toilets instead of squatting behind a wagon or a bush. Sometimes we'll have to travel on paved roads where the original trail crosses grain fields, or developed property. D'you two want to be part of my wagon crew?"

"You've gotta be crazy, Allen. Me, ride in a steel-wheeled wagon … for two hundred miles? No way! Absolutely not!"

I'd hated the few times I had to ride home from school in a grain-wagon. If the horses walked it was slow and boring; if they trotted the wagon rattled and bounced, jolting me about until I was sure all my bones would be shaken out of their sockets. If I hadn't drunk the milk in my lunch pail at noon there would be butter floating in it when I got home. No covered wagons for me, thank you very much. And I didn't give a damn if 250 other people were going. Or thirty covered wagons. If they all wanted to be crazy that was no skin off my face.

"But Mary, you don't understand. Each prairie schooner is allowed to have two outriders … to act as … well, whatever." Allen's mouth beneath his beard wore a craggy grin.

"Oh!" That put an entirely different perspective on the idea. Clarence didn't like riding. If he could tolerate travelling in the wagon maybe this was our chance to share an entirely new experience. We were heading into semi-retirement. What better way to kick it off than by doing something outlandish?

I turned questioning eyes on my husband as I refilled his tea-cup. "How do you feel about travelling for two weeks in a steel-wheeled wagon? Putting up a tent every night, sleeping in it, crawling in and out of the thing until you get the feeling you're an old bear and it's your den, then striking it every morning and packing it into the wagon for another long day's travel? You'll be eating sourdough pancakes and beans and whatever else can be cooked for nine people over a two-burner camp stove. No radios. Certainly no telephones. Not even a comfortable chair to sit on, just feed bales and wooden stools ... or perhaps the wagon pole if the team is unhitched. And of course there'll be mosquitoes. Always mosquitoes."

Clarence's grin was thoughtful. "It might be fun."

Allen Murdoch was a great story teller. His health wasn't good so he'd need lots of help from all of us with his outfit. But he would keep his wagon passengers well entertained during the long dusty miles.

Before Murdoch left the next day we had agreed to be part of his crew of nine when the train pulled out of Moose Jaw on the morning of June 21, 1982. I'd be riding my own horse, as would Florence, a Saskatchewan lady who would be the other outrider for the Murdoch wagon. Allen planned to take his saddle horse too, so if any of the wagon folk wanted to ride for a spell they could. However, that idea didn't turn out the way he had intended.

The Murdoch wagon would be "home" for two weeks to nine people who, apart from having Allen as a mutual friend, would be total strangers to each other until they met at the beginning of the trek. Could we adjust to the rigours of life as it was one hundred years ago while living cheek-to-jowl with people we had never seen before, sharing everything from tents to camp duties? Or would we be clawing at each others throats the second day out?

Each wagon was to be the stable for the horses connected with it. They would spend their nights tied to its wheels. For the Murdoch outfit this meant five horses would be sharing four wheels. This didn't sound like too bad an arrangement, provided none of the animals began throwing their heels around. Allen said his bay team could be tied to the same wheel without fighting, but his pinto saddle mare, who saw herself as head honcho, must have a wheel to herself. And she needed it. I was to find out that Allen's horses were all shod with heavy iron shoes with long vicious corks, which could inflict lethal damage to another animal if they ever landed a kick, or to a human if they stepped on your foot. Murdoch had gone to considerable trouble to have his animals shod that way because he said that was the heavy style horseshoes the early pioneers would have used. And he wanted to be authentic.

With Murdoch's three animals tied on one side of the wagon that meant the two outriders' horses would each have a separate wheel on the opposite side of the wagon. That sounded acceptable enough at the time, because the possibility that Murdoch's wagon might end up with six horses and that two strange horses would be expected to share a wheel *and* their feed never entered my head.

But what horse should I ride? Dark Velvet, Khem's daugher out of Shasta? I'd be devastated if she got a damaging kick. And being a mare she was more apt to be fidgety around strange horses than a gelding. Gelding? Hmm? Eldorado?

He *was* a good walker. Wagons' teams would seldom go off a walk. So why not?

Eldorado and I began putting in miles that spring. I used any excuse to ride him. Checking for calves, weak spots in fences, moving cattle to other pastures, riding fields to find out which ones were dry enough to cultivate, carrying out lunches. Poisoning gophers—doesn't sound like something you'd do from a horse's back? It turned out amazingly well .... As did taking the grain and fertilizer trucks to the field for the men. I'd lead Eldorado through the open truck window until we got to where the vehicle was to be left, then I'd ride him home.

When we loaded him into our horse trailer on June 19 and left to meet up with Allen's outfit, and the other outrider's horse (they were all to be trailered to Moose Jaw from Murdoch's farm the next day), Eldorado was fit. A thousand miles wouldn't have fazed him ... unless his shoes gave trouble. He had never been shod before.

Eldorado was a level-headed, sensible horse. Even so, I was glad that before leaving the Murdoch farm Allen decided he'd hitch up his team of bays for one last practice run. By now they were quite accustomed to seeing the swaying white canvas top flapping behind them, but that was something that had taken considerable time and a wreck or two to bring about. I didn't expect Eldorado to fly into a dither, but if he did I'd rather he do it here than in Moose Jaw's morning rush-hour traffic.

For the first few minutes Eldorado watched the canvas top with every muscle triggered to fire. He was more than half convinced it was something alive, something waiting to flutter down and "get him," but as soon as he decided it was safe he relaxed and from then on it was old-hat.

When we got back to the Murdoch yard following the practice run I decided I'd ride a bit farther before unsaddling. Eldorado immediately figured we were heading home and was in a hurry to get there. I laughed, and patted his neck. "You'll never get home going that way, old fella. You've got your directions mixed up." I learned later it was I, not the horse, whose sense of direction had gone haywire.

Eldorado was so homesick that first night I strung a rope across the back of his stall, and still made a late-night check to make sure Murdoch's barn door was properly shut. I didn't want to wake up in the morning to find my horse gone.

The next night all the trekkers' horses (over two hundred) were stabled in an exhibition barn in Moose Jaw. But that night I wasn't worried about Eldorado running off and leaving me. He had struck up a friendship with the quarter-horse mare he had travelled down with in the Murdoch trailer. Now that he had a sense of belonging he wouldn't leave ... not even if he was turned loose.

The grounds of Moose Jaw's Western Development Museum were an ant-hill of activity as the first rays of a sun eager to get started on this, its longest run of the year, rose above the horizon.

Horses, fed and watered before sun-up, were being harnessed and saddled and held in restless readiness for the "hitch-up" call. Tents were struck and packed inside the thirty-plus covered wagons by men and women who appeared to have stepped right out of the prairie-wool era of days long gone.

The Colony Trek of 1982, duplicating the trek of one hundred years earlier, was about to get under way.

The banquet, the speeches, the send-off festivities of the night before were past. Now it was down to the serious business of getting thirty-some covered wagons, their accompanying outriders, several democrats and open buggies, plus a cabal of mounted scouts through Moose Jaw's morning rush-hour traffic without incident, and safely on the first leg of their 180-mile trek into history.

Anyone seeing the display of covered wagons standing hub-to-hub, sparkling in fresh paint and new canvas tops, and the excited horses, skittish and restless at the strangeness of it all, drivers and their helpers too tense themselves to have any real calming effect on their nervous charges, couldn't fail but realize the potential for trouble.

The atmosphere was so charged with electricity that normally staid teams, unable to handle the waiting, began rearing and lunging. Even Eldorado was dancing like a wind-whipped leaf in a hurry to escape its branch.

It seemed almost inevitable that a major mix-up was skulking in the shadows waiting for a chance to happen, an accident that would cast a pall over the trek, perhaps doom it before it was properly started. Could all these skittish teams settle down enough to get their wagons under way in an orderly fashion when drivers were given the go-ahead by trail bosses?

As the shouted command "Wagons Ho" rang through the morning air, tensions mushroomed and spread with the speed of electricity surging along wires, as first one outfit then another was signalled to roll out and take its designated place. Each outfit was to follow the wagon immediately preceding it.

When a wagon moved out and into position so did the outriders belonging to it. Some riders were asked to travel behind their wagons, others rode beside the teams, hoping to calm down and give some reassurance to horses who in most cases had never travelled far beyond their own farm gate.

Thanks to good organization, firm commands from wagon bosses, and complete co-operation from the drivers and their helpers, the wagon train left Moose Jaw's exhibition grounds without a snarl-up.

Promptly at 7:30 on this, and every other morning, the call "Wagons Ho" saw the lead wagon moving. Then the others like a giant snake fell into line, each in its designated place, to writhe steadily towards its final destination.

Moose Jaw traffic stopped as the wagon train moved through the city. Smiles and greetings from motorists waiting along the way told us few minded the possibility of arriving late for work that morning. They were witnessing a piece of history.

Mounted scouts rode up and down the length of the train which stretched for well over half a mile. They were checking to see if any wagon was having a problem. Slower outfits were ordered to close up the gaps. And so the prairie schooners rumbled on.

The city skyline faded, pavement was exchanged for side roads, horses became more accustomed to the creaking of wagons and the flapping of canvas tops. The day got hot. The trek to Saskatoon had begun.

Not being a sun worshipper, I was glad to ride in the shade of our covered wagon for the rest of the morning. At first Florence, the other outrider with our outfit, scoffed at me in her snappish ex-teacherish manner, "If you don't like the sun you should have stayed home." A short time later she was trying, unsuccessfully, to coax her buckskin quarter horse into moving close enough to the flapping canvas so she too could benefit from its shade.

Western hats were pulled low to shield faces from the sizzling sun, *Paba* lotions were dragged from saddle bags and applied liberally. But still faces burned. Harness horses, many with too little conditioning, were soon dripping with sweat. Those of us who liked horses availed ourselves of every rest stop to bathe not just shoulders but the animals' bodies and legs as well.

At first Jerry, a stout-hearted bay on the Murdoch wagon, took a dim view of getting sloshed with water. But before the day was over he was nickering if he felt in danger of being overlooked.

Wagon occupants reported the covered wagons amazingly cool and comfortable. But too bumpy to read or write or knit, things some trekkers had hoped to do.

The first day outriders were asked to stay beside their own wagons in case the teams gave trouble. After that riders could range up and down the length of the train, visiting with other riders and wagon folks as we wished.

Three Mounties, in 1882 uniforms, led the procession in and out of cities and towns. At other times they fell back to visit with wagon folk and outriders. The tales of their experiences both in and out of the Force brought out some great discussions. Discussions that livened up many a dusty mile and sometimes engendered comments like "My God! I'd hate to be a rapist if you girls were on the bench. But I must say this: there would certainly be no repeat offenders."

The Murdoch wagon was heavy and the team was young, so those who travelled in it were anxious to do everything they could to make things easier for them. On the hills everyone but the driver got out of the wagon and walked. Sometimes they pushed. When feet got blistered and bunions hurt, people still walked. I overheard one elderly trekker remark to her equally elderly friend:

"You know Esther, I really don't mind all this walking. Nor the pushing. When I stop to think about it, I think I actually rather enjoy it. It makes me feel more in tune with the pioneer women of a hundred years ago, gives me a sense of having closer kinship with them. Because they must have walked a lot, had blisters, and been tired too, yet for them it wasn't a lark that would end in two weeks. They had no comfortable homes waiting for them, no modern conveniences to go back to. This *was* their life."

Evelyn Boon almost seemed to be talking to herself as she continued. "It was the courage and the dedication of those women who came west with their men to help wrestle a living from an untamed and hostile land that laid the foundation for what we have today."

Then after a moment she turned to her daughter with a mischievous twinkle in her eyes. "You know, Jo-Anne, we were told the goal of this trek was to re-live the experiences, get the real feeling of what it was like to be a pioneer, well, I think we're beginning to get it."

I began leading Eldorado so one or other of the walkers could ride him for a spell and rest their blistered feet.

Esther Mainland was a city lady nearing seventy who had never been on a horse before, but she had the true pioneer spirit and was game to give it a try. Like the other women in the wagons she wore the long full skirt, apron and sunbonnet of another era. Hampered by this sort of cumbersome garb anyone could have had trouble getting into the saddle, but we encouraged her. "You can do it, Esther. We'll help you."

Eldorado, looking as if this might be expecting rather a lot from a horse, braced himself with a resigned expression on his face. Then he'd heave a sigh that seemed to say, "Well, *okay*, I won't move, but someone had better hold down the right stirrup or she'll pull my saddle sideways."

Esther managed to haul herself up into the saddle with a lot of help—boosting from behind, pulling from in front, and vocal encouragement from all directions, plus an outstanding display of patience from a horse.

Once mounted, the business of getting her skirts and petticoats untangled from around her boots took top priority. Then her sunbonnet had to be straightened, her apron adjusted. Only then, when both hands were clamped around the saddle horn in a grip that would have taken a sledge hammer to loosen, did she signal she was ready to start.

It took a slight tug on the halter to convince Eldorado it really was *okay* now if he moved. Even though he walked so carefully he might have been picking his way through Waterford glass, I don't think the lady enjoyed her equestrian experience. But others enjoyed riding him.

As the days passed some horses got badly scalded shoulders, others had saddle sores—mostly because of insufficient conditioning. The whole venture was a breeze for Eldorado. Often he was the only horse in the entire train who didn't show a wet hair except under the saddle blanket. And not always there. People lining roadsides to watch the trek rumble past would call out. "How do you do it, lady? *Your* horse looks fresh as a daisy."

It wasn't because I had been trying to be easy on him. I rode up and down the length of the train many times every day. Spread out as the wagons were (sometimes as much as a mile), teamsters appreciated getting messages about planned rest stops from the leaders up front. Eldorado was one of the saddle horses who travelled considerably farther than the 20 to 25 creaking miles the train went each day.

Something I hadn't really appreciated until now was Eldorado's disposition. Some of the trek horses would let fly with both heels the moment another animal got within range. Not Eldorado. Such a thought never entered his head. He didn't even object when asked to share a wagon wheel and his oat bucket with a strange horse.

Visitors, often with no idea a horse might be dangerous, strolled around our evening campsites to talk, to reminisce, or just to watch as trekkers went about their camp chores. There was something about my Arabian gelding that made children gravitate to him like flies around a honey pot. He was always getting hugged and petted. Any part of his anatomy would do. Front or back, top or bottom, it didn't matter. Just as long as it was something they could get their arms around or their hands on.

Not all horses were so agreeable. One animal put his owner in hospital. Another bit his driver's hand. A team of mules had to wear trip ropes; a saddle horse fought his rider for the entire trek. Still others had roped-off areas behind them to keep folks a safe distance from their heels.

I often draped the reins on Eldorado's neck and jotted memos in a notebook as we travelled. Sometimes I'd dismount to try for a better picture of the wagons coming behind. I'd flip the reins over the saddle to free both hands, then walk backwards watching for the exact shot I hoped for. Eldorado stayed right beside me, stopping and starting when I did, trotting if I turned to run a few yards to get ahead for a better background shot.

A lady who had been watching from her wagon leaned out to ask, "The way your horse always stays right beside you—did you teach him to do that? Like training a dog to heel?"

I laughed and patted Eldorado's neck. "No. Maybe he just figures it's what he's supposed to do."

She threw the gelding a wistful look and sighed, "He sure is nice. I think I might ride if I had a horse like that."

One of the Suffolk Punch mares pulling the wagon a couple of outfits behind Murdoch's wagon had a foal at foot. The little guy got so attached to Eldorado that at campsites it wasn't unusual to see him hanging around the Murdoch wagon, helping Eldorado eat his oats.

One evening a lady whose delicate skin tones and expensively tailored suit spelled "city" gushed to the man beside her, "Look, dear. A mare and foal. Aren't they sweet?"

"Don't be silly, Madge. That's not a mare. It's a gelding."

She watched thoughtfully for a few minutes, then, looking as if she had just swallowed a rather large dose of enlightenment, murmured, "D'you know, dear, I never knew geldings had colts."

A muffled explosion from behind the wagon where Murdoch was mending a piece of harness said he might be choking to death.

With the trek receiving national attention on television and in the daily newspapers, it was inevitable that interest in us should grow. Each day saw progressively bigger crowds lining the roadsides to watch us pass. Some came for hundreds of miles to cheer and wave encouragement.

Perhaps they shared the feelings of the couple who remarked to me, "We watch for you folks every night on the news. With so much trouble in the world, hearing how you trekkers are coping, living under rugged conditions yet so obviously having a good time doing it, brings a ray of brightness into our lives."

We outriders had the advantage of being able to stop whenever we chose to talk with people along the roadside. Wagons couldn't; it would have held up the rest of the train.

Whenever I stopped, children crowded around Eldorado. Some thought it was an adventure just to pat his velvety muzzle, others were starry-eyed in hopes of a ride. I frequently took them up in the saddle with me for a short walk-around, or for their parents to snap a picture. There must be hundreds of pictures scattered around the country of an Arabian with a coat like polished copper and a white stripe down his face.

Water and feed trucks were brought in every evening and parked at our campsite overnight, as were toilets on wheels. Water and toilet-trucks showed up again at the noon break. The arrival of the "wee hoose" caused an immediate line-up. At any other time the call of nature had to be answered as best it could. One of the lead wagons towed a toilet-on-wheels that women, and men too, travelling near the front of the trek were welcome to use. It was too far from the wagons farther back in the train to be of any help. Riders were lucky if they could find a hill or bush to squat behind. There were places in flat Saskatchewan where that was impossible.

One day Evelyn and Esther, looking as if they had discovered a diamond of the first water, beckoned me over. "Mary, we think we've come up with a great idea."

My eyebrows arched into a question. I rode closer to the wagon's end-gate to hear more from the women leaning out over it. After shooting a hasty over-the-shoulder look to make sure no men were listening, Evelyn's voice lowered to a conspiratorial whisper.

"There's no reason why we women in the wagons towards the back of the train should have to hang on to our pee, praying bladders won't burst before the 'wee hoose' shows up. We should improvise, but we'll need your help. And we'll need your horse too."

So it was that now when the train stopped to give the teams a few minutes' rest, the women from the last half-dozen wagons would move systematically to the back of the train, warning their males to "keep your eyes front." Then I'd dismount and stand Eldorado between them and oncoming traffic in such a way that when a woman spread her long skirt as if preparing to mount, and another stood directly behind the gelding, the occupant of the on-site rest-room squatting close to Eldorado's right legs was completely invisible to passers-by. Suddenly the prestige of travelling in the lead wagons lost a lot of its appeal. At least for the women passengers.

On a day so hot that stinkweed wilted in the summerfallow, I stopped to ask roadside folk how far, and which way, to the nearest town. The Murdoch wagon needed bread, and I planned to ride in and get it.

"Four miles. And that's too far for you to ride and then have to carry groceries all the way back when it's so hot. Anyway it's a half-holiday; the store won't be open. But I tell you what. I know the lady who runs it. I'll drive in, pick up what you need, and bring it to your campsite this evening."

On another occasion a couple, hearing our bread supply was again low and I was planning to ride for more, wouldn't hear of it. "No, no. You must be tired of eating store-bought bread. You just wait. Molly and I'll go home and bake a batch of homemade bread for you." That evening they showed up with three loaves of the finest-tasting bread I ever hope to eat, and to make it a feast fit for a king they also brought a pound of home-made butter. They refused to hear of our paying for it.

People were always wanting to do things for us. Perhaps because those who made up the Murdoch outfit were all old-timers, 64 years or older ... except for Jo-Anne, our "baby." She was twenty-something. Our most senior senior was a gentleman well up in his eighties who had come all the way from England to share in the trek experience. (Another wagon had a couple from Australia among their passengers.) Other trekkers called our wagon the "happy oldies," but the epithet 'happy' could easily have applied to many others on the trip. Most folks were friendly and cheerful, and like true pioneers, eager to help fellow travellers in any way they could.

It might be a sun-bonneted lady leaning from her wagon to offer a cool drink to a parched rider she didn't know. It might be scouts using their saddle horses and lassos to help tired teams up steep hills. It might be willing hands pitching in to help re-set a wagon tire, replace a cast shoe, or mend a piece of broken harness. It might be the friendly voice calling, "I'll carry that water bucket for you, ma'am," when your arms were beginning to feel as if they had separated from their sockets. (Water had to be carried to the horses, and sometimes it seemed we must be trying to tank up camels.) Or it might be a rider trotting back down the length of the train calling "rest stop" to frustrated drivers wondering "What's this stop for?"

Then there was the night that rain threatening to flood our tents sent trekkers scurrying to an empty hayloft through ankle-deep gumbo. Sleeping in a hayloft was another "first" for many of us.

Rain had been impending all afternoon. Tents were pitched, horses fed, and suppers gulped before the skies cracked and water poured out. In minutes the campsite, which had been rock-hard clay, turned into a morass of mud that stuck to feet and came up in man-sized chunks every time a foot was raised.

The men tried to ditch water away from the tents, but it was so flat there was no place for it to go. Wet stains on the tent floors spread steadily inwards. It looked like a bad night until word came: "Trekkers are welcome to sleep in my hayloft."

There was a general exodus of bedraggled figures staggering under sleeping blankets and foamies, one of the few luxuries (apart from the offer of a hayloft) we had over our predecessors, who probably slept under their wagons on flour-sacks stuffed with prairie wool.

It was the first time I'd slept in a hayloft and the thought of mice was disturbing. Even more disturbing was the overpowering smell of pigs that came up an air shaft close to my face. I was wondering sourly to Clarence which was the better way to die, stay in the hayloft and asphyxiate, or go back to the tent and drown? He smiled quietly, as if it was too late to do either properly. "Listen, Princess, try switching ends. Put your face where your feet are."

Ye Gods! Why hadn't I thought of that. It was so simple.

That rain brought a change in the weather. From then on mornings found everything in the tents so damp and clammy that getting dressed brought nostalgic thoughts of home. However, by going to bed with our clothes on and sometimes donning a Siwash sweater as well, we slept comfortably. And it made getting up a lot simpler.

Mornings came early on the trek. The official "wakie-wakie" was at 5:30, but few trekkers were still abed when it sounded. The first grey light of dawn always saw some early riser crawl sleepily from his tent.

The moment he did his horses greeted him with an eager whinny ... a greeting that snowballed until every horse in camp was neighing for his breakfast. That was the signal for people to crawl from tents like ants from a disturbed ant-hill.

Soon cheerfully called "good mornings" bounced like echoes back and forth across the campgrounds. The sound of contentedly munching horses, the tantalizing aroma of freshly brewed coffee, and bacon frying in the pan, coaxed even the worst sleepy-head into exchanging her snug cocoon for the big world outside. It was a matter of pride—no wagon wanted to keep the train waiting when the 7:30 call "Wagons Ho" slivered the morning air. And no wagon ever did.

It was always a welcome change when a community treated the trekkers to a deluxe meal, as they frequently did, but we ate well all the time.

Each wagon was responsible for its own food. With two good cooks looking after the Murdoch crew, we enjoyed gourmet stews, feather-light dumplings, steamed can-bread, sourdough biscuits, canned venison, and even the fruit of the cactus berry ... which, for folks like me who had never heard of it, looks like a big green gooseberry and has a mild gooseberry flavour. The noon meal was usually sandwiches and fresh fruit ... provided I'd had a successful "buffalo hunt" in some adjacent town.

The extreme heat at the start of the trek that had scorched faces and brought saddle sores and blistered shoulders to some of the animals was whirled away one morning on a cold wind sharp enough to slice bark off trees. It whipped up soil, mixed it with just enough moisture to make it stick, then flung it in a shrieking fury against the wagon train.

The wagons' white canvas tops quickly turned a murky grey. Faces leathered by the sun became drifted over with topsoil that turned tiny wrinkles into dirt-filled ravines. Eyes and noses on riders and horses alike were encrusted with layers of dirt. Hair escaping from under hastily wrapped scarves became stiff as witches' tresses. Those of us at the end of the train fared the worst. We had been swallowing additional dust blown back on us from the lead wagons all morning.

And that was the day I volunteered to ride and get groceries for a wagon whose elderly couple didn't have an outrider to run their errands.

When Eldorado trotted briskly down the town's main street I was glad to see a couple of seniors who were pleased to hold my horse. (Hitching posts and paved streets don't go hand in hand. Not in Saskatchewan.) Apart from this couple the town seemed deserted. Everyone must have gone out to see the wagon train.

In the store I made the mistake of glancing in a mirror (something the ladies in our tent didn't have and rarely bothered to borrow). Great Jumping Horned Toads! Was that me? It looked like the face of one of the fiends who stoke the fires of hell.

I grabbed the sack of groceries, threw some money on the counter, and rushed out to my horse. Back among fellow trekkers I mightn't be quite so conspicuous. Here in town everyone looked so clean ....

My escape wasn't to be that easy. Eldorado was surrounded by townsfolk who had come out of the woodwork to pet and admire him. But even better than petting a trekker's horse is talking to its rider. Suddenly the way I looked no longer seemed important.

When I took side trips like this it was never any trouble to catch up with the slow-moving train again.

Both my horse and I welcomed the chance to move out a bit faster because sometimes we found keeping to a walk, hour after hour, monotonous. I even learned to cat-nap in the saddle.

When the trek reached the community pasture and the Indian reserve things looked up for me, as well as for other riders who didn't mind putting on a few extra miles. Now we could canter off to various high hills, each affording a fantastic view of the train as it came and went.

One day we travelled terrain so rugged the driver of the water truck told us, "The road ahead is so bad I won't be able to bring the water truck in for your noon stop. Each wagon should carry whatever water they need with them."

We had been so busy tanking up for our equine friends at that watering stop we had neglected to refill our own container. It looked like a long drought for the Murdoch crew.

A fellow trekker who knew we were low on water rode over to say, "There's a good spring within a mile or so of the wagon trail. I'm heading over there now to refill my canteen. Want to come with me, Mary?"

Do bees like honey?

But I couldn't carry a five-gallon water barrel. What else was there in the wagon? Esther and Evelyn made a quick search, but the only thing they could come up with was an ice-cream pail we had used to bathe the team's sweaty shoulders. And it didn't have a lid. I grabbed it anyway and followed my companion at an easy lope. The pail could be washed out at the spring (by now we were no longer squeamish—if it came to dipping water for brushing teeth from a horse bucket or walking a quarter of a mile for a fresh supply, we were apt to dip from the horse bucket).

The spring was easy to find. After giving our horses

and ourselves a drink of the sparkling water, and washing out and filling our containers, we decided to head off across country to intercept the train at some as-yet undetermined spot.

It was sand-blow-out country with scrub brush, creeping cedar, steep gullies, and equally sharp cactus-studded inclines, some of them quite high. It was challenging riding up and down, dodging trees, and trying not to slop water out of the coverless pail.

After some time our horses climbed sharply to the top of what I supposed was merely an unusually high hill. As we crested it my heart did a flip-flop. The hill had disappeared.

In its place was a narrow path that wound around between a sheer drop to a sand pit some thirty feet below on one side, and a perilous precipice ablaze with yellow cactus blossoms on the other. Ahead the path was an almost vertical descent through sand that slid and shifted uneasily as the horses waded through it.

After traversing what seemed like a ribbon festooned across the top of the world, Eldorado slithered down the steep descent as easily as would one of his desert ancestors. In no time I was handing the ice-cream pail, miraculously still two-thirds full, in through the back of the wagon to its thirsty—and surprised—passengers. It seems they had been laying odds as to whether I'd have any water left by the time I rejoined them.

When the trek was coming into Douglas Park on Lake Diefenbaker the wagons had to come down a cliff before crossing a steep gully. Men had to drag logs into the gulch, then cover them with sand to make a "bridge" for the wagons. Now they were shovelling sand onto the logs like excited dogs digging out gophers.

I knew the wagons were to come over the same cliff I had just ridden down, bringing shovels for the men, and I was worried that some of them, top-heavy as they were, might tip forward and upset. Eldorado, even with his haunches well under him, had slithered and half-slid on the steepest part. Several other horses had been ridden over it since then but it still looked too steep for wagons.

When the first outfit started down I was almost too scared to watch. It pitched dangerously forwards and seemed about to topple over onto the backs of the horses. But they were a strong, steady team that knew how to lean well back into their breechings, then ahead into their collars as the wagon lurched first down, then up the sharp incline on the other side. That wagon had made it safely. Everyone cheered the lady driver.

Before other wagons were allowed to follow, shovels were again used, this time to cut away the sharpness of the cliff. Each wagon cut down the sand still more, making the descent progressively less perilous. However, I was glad I wasn't in a wagon. (I get goose bumps the size of grapefruit it I drive a tractor over a little side-hill.)

It was while the wagons were at Douglas Park that another horse was brought in to team up with Allen's pinto mare, who had been used to spell off one of the Murdoch bays. With heavy going ahead Allen had decided to go to a four-horse hitch.

He knew, as did every other teamster on the trek, that the new mare was potential trouble. The high-topped prairie schooners, the crowds, the excitement ... she had rarely been off the farm, and now to find herself among all this, teamed up with strange horses and an unfamiliar driver, could throw her into a panic. If that panic spread to the bays (or even if it didn't) the Murdoch outfit could get out of control, wrecking not only their own wagon, but any others that happened to be in their path.

All the other wagons hitched up hurriedly and pulled well out of the way. The mounted scouts rode up, ropes uncoiled, their horses tense and waiting. The riders, all big, powerful men, built like battleships, looked just as well qualified to control a rambunctious animal as did their heavily muscled mounts. Yet it was Eldorado who was beside the new mare when she started up.

The chestnut mare, after spending the night tied alongside Eldorado, saw him as the only friend she had in this strange new world, but even so it came as a total surprise when Allen said, "I think you boys better stay back. Wait a bit. Mary's little Arabian is awfully sensible and the mare seems to have taken quite a liking to him, so I've a notion if he's beside her she'll act better than if you fellows on your big horses try to take over. If Mary doesn't mind riding at the mare's head, that's the way I think we ought to start out. And we'll see what happens."

My adrenalin was working overtime, my hands felt clammy, but I tried to keep my voice low and confident as I crooned reassurance to a mare who was looking ready to fly apart if a worm sneezed. Eldorado reached out to her and for a brief moment their noses touched.

When the three Murdoch horses started up as if pulling a covered wagon was as ordinary as eating grass, and Eldorado, the horse she saw as a friend, wasn't scared either, the new mare began to settle down. The hopping and dancing soon gave way to a flat-footed walk, the terrified glitter faded from her eyes, and she was on the way to becoming a welcome addition to our outfit.

A wave of relief spread like a gentle breeze over the trekkers as they watched the Murdoch wagon circle the open area a couple of times, then fall into line in its proper place and wait for the call "Wagons Ho." The ladies of our wagon immediately re-christened the mare "Honey," and the name stuck.

I have great respect and admiration for all those people who travelled in the wagons. There were times when I'd have been scared spitless if I'd been in their place—the morning Honey became one of the Murdoch horses, the day the wagons had to come down the steep banks prior to Douglas Park. Yet I never ever heard any-one—man, woman or child—cry "Stop! Let me out. I want to walk." Obviously I'd have made a poor pioneer.

Most evenings there was entertainment for the trekkers to go to, provided either by professionals or by some of the more talented trekkers. But many of us found ourselves so tired that keeping eyes from closing and heads from nodding became an embarrassment, so we usually skipped the entertainment and spent the time grooming the horses, scything grass to give them a special treat, or preparing sourdough for the morning pancakes. And always there was water to carry for the horses. They seemed to have a perpetual thirst. Perhaps because they knew it had to be carried in buckets.

With the horses fed and comfortable we might relax a while and chat with visitors or neighbouring wagoners before getting ourselves cleaned up and into bed, ready for another early rise.

Most of us enjoyed the luxury of a warm sponge-bath in our tent every night. It didn't seem at all strange to have a woman you hadn't known until a few days ago scrubbing your back.

As soon as Murdoch's second outrider discovered there were other quarter horse aficionados travelling in the lead wagons, we didn't see much of her. Sometimes she showed up to sleep in our tent, but mostly she did-n't. Had she been half as amiable as her quarter-horse mare we would have missed her more. Nevertheless I felt sorry for her. The other eight people attached to the Murdoch wagon all got along famously, whereas she didn't appear to like any of us, and no one quite knew why.

There was no shortage of challenge on the trek. Some hills were so sharp that before starting down, ropes had to be strung from wagon-reach back to saddle horses to help slow the wagon's progress. Other hills were so long and so steep that sometimes straining teams gave up and stood with heaving sides and drooping heads, waiting for help.

Wagons like this were potential disaster. If one began rolling back and the tired team couldn't hold it, and if (as sometimes happened) wagons behind had stopped nose-to-endgate on a trail so boxed in with trees that even a saddle horse had troubling squeezing past, the pile-up could have been horrendous.

At times like this snatch teams stationed at the top of the hill were invaluable. But sometimes these teams caused trouble. One day a driver who had momentarily dropped the lines heard a warning shout and looked up to see his Belgians disappearing over the horizon. Luck-ily scouts got the runaways back and the trek proceeded.

Sometimes only quick action prevented an acci-dent. Jerry, one of the young lead horses on the Mur-doch wagon, got a back leg over his traces during a rest stop and the driver started the team without noticing it. Jerry was quiet enough about most things, but a breech-ing or any piece of harness touching his back legs was his bugaboo. This time, when he flew into a wild fren-zy of kicking and lunging, a nearby scout quickly saved the situation from getting worse by grabbing Jerry's head and snubbing it up tight against his saddle horse until someone was able to get the trace undone.

Jerry didn't like railway crossings either. He thought jumping them was the only way to deal with them, so I began riding Eldorado at his head whenever one was coming up, until he learned to cross them in a more orthodox manner.

The day the wagon train pulled into Elbow, the town welcomed trekkers with hot dogs, juice and coffee as well as shady trees where we could sit and relax while visiting with the townsfolk. Horses had been quickly unhitched and tied to wagons parked alongside a railway track, with no thought given to what would happen should a train suddenly come blasting through town. When the roar and rattle of a through-freight reached the trekkers' ears they leaped up and raced back to their teams in time to see horses lunging and rearing. Some had already broken loose.

A rider coming back from checking on her mount hurried over to me. "I'm glad our horses were tied near your gelding because when my horse Scout saw your little Arab was still eating he must have thought the train couldn't be all that bad. Otherwise I'm sure he'd have broken his halter. And he's the very devil to catch." A rail line crosses our ranch, so trains were nothing new to Eldorado.

No vehicle on rubber was allowed within the campsite. But that didn't stop visitors. They walked in. And the closer we got to Saskatoon the larger the crowds became. Now there were so many people swarming around as we went about our evening chores that Jo-Anne looked up from grooming Jerry one evening and hissed, "I'm beginning to feel like an animal in the zoo."

Not long before that Evelyn had whispered to me, sotto voce, "I don't mind visitors. In fact I really do like them; I just wish they wouldn't stand and stare when I'm washing my false teeth." Esther reported she had been resting in the tent she and her husband shared when someone lifted the flap and looked inside. "Lucky you weren't having a sponge-bath," I laughed. We did feel that this was an unnecessary (and perhaps unthinking) invasion of our privacy.

Well-wishers had been plentiful along the entire route, but nearing Saskatoon the crowds increased at an alarming rate. People arriving from various Canadian provinces as well as from the United States and parts of Europe caused Evelyn to quip, "I think I've almost perfected my queenly wave, but I'm afraid my smile looks frozen." Indeed, royalty could not have been given a more enthusiastic welcome.

With crowds packing every available space on either side of the road, teamsters were nervously aware of the havoc a frightened team could cause. Outriders rode close in case of trouble, but the watchers seemed blissfully unaware of any potential danger.

I was riding stirrup to collar with the young lead mare on Murdoch's wagon when a cyclist whizzed past so close he brushed my outside stirrup. Eldorado didn't twitch a muscle, but horses farther up the line weren't so unflappable. One animal reared, then fell and got himself and his mate into a tangle. We were held up for some time on account of it.

A driver still farther up the road gave the cyclist a sharp clip with the end of a line as he raced past, and that ended the episode of the cyclist.

Most trekkers from Saskatchewan were expecting to see some of their family and friends waving to them as we approached Saskatoon. Clarence and I didn't expect to see anyone we knew. So it was a big boost to my ego when time and time again I heard someone call out, "Oh, there she is!" and I would see folks I'd chatted with along the route waving and yelling congratulations as if we were long-time friends. It gave me a nice warm feeling of belonging.

Then when the train had to stop for traffic up ahead, I nearly fell out of the saddle when I heard someone beside me say "Hello, Grandma." It was my young grandson, Michael Lea, and behind him were his parents, Heather and John Lea. They had come from their home near Winnipeg to welcome Clarence and me into Saskatoon, and what a lovely surprise that was. It completely made my day. And it made Michael's too. He didn't just ride a trekker's horse, he rode in a covered wagon ... with his Grandpa.

Saskatoon police worked hard to keep people from crowding too close to wagons and teams that didn't quite know what to make of so much excitement. Yet to my knowledge there were no serious mishaps on the trip.

That, afternoon when wagons were unhitched for the last time, goodbyes were said with sadness, but it was a sadness tempered with the pride of accomplishment ... the same pride trekkers of another era must have felt on achieving their goal. We had reached back into history, accomplished what we set out to do, and enjoyed doing it. *and* we had made lifelong friends.

The Colony Trek of '82 was an experience those who shared it will never forget.

As for Eldorado, he won a lot of respect for a breed sometimes thought of as the millionaires' status symbol. Many admired him, some tried to buy him, others pointed him out as the perfect candidate for competitive riding. I didn't tell them his sister had foaled an International Champion Competitive Trail Horse ... and that a twelve-year-old had ridden him to victory.

Back at the ranch, Eldorado was turned out to pasture, but I no longer thought of him as the last chick out of its shell.

Chapter Fourteen

A Bit of Hollywood

Hollywood? Coming here? To this ranch? To take pictures of our musk oxen? For the *Clan of the Cave Bear* movie? I had never in my wildest dreams imagined anything like this happening. Nor had I ever imagined the horse I once said looked like a chick too late out of its shell was to play a part in the filming of that movie.

Ordinarily when Clarence wanted to see the musk oxen he drove out in the pick-up, called them, and they came to him. Now, because there must be no wheel tracks for the cameras to pick up, and because movie Director Jack Couffer's penchant for excellence made it important he knew the exact angle the musk oxen would be approaching the cameras, he and Couffer had to walk to locate the musk oxen. Then when the filming began, my husband walked again, this time with the musk oxen following him. He needed to get them to the exact spot where hunters so prehistoric they hadn't yet mastered the rudiments of speech could jump out of hiding and pretend to be chasing them so the cameras in the blind could film it. The musk oxen seemed to understand that this was play-acting, some sort of silly human game. But what the heck, they didn't mind playing it. They never hesitated about coming back to do it again when Clarence called them. But I was becoming more worried. My husband, a brittle diabetic nearing 70, shouldn't be doing so much walking. Yet he always assured me, "I'll be all right." I knew I couldn't be any help when it came to getting the musk oxen to the filming area. But I could ride out earlier and locate which bush they were in. A horse doesn't leave tracks.

I had been using Fantasy for ranch work and pleasure riding, but she wasn't the horse for this job. When asked to stop and stand she would soon get restless and start whinnying. That was something I definitely didn't need. So I decided I'd better ride Eldorado. He was more apt to stand quietly and not draw attention to himself, because if he did it was almost sure to bring the musk oxen out of whichever bush they were in to investigate. And since Kivy, a musk-ox cow, had learned she could scare horses by thundering towards them at a snorting, stamping, ground-punishing charge, that had become her preferred method of investigating. When musk oxen are hurtling towards them in a stiff-legged Attila-the-Hun charge, no animal with half a brain is going to hang around to argue.

Clarence always maintained "Kivy wouldn't have hit them. It's just a game." Maybe. But the horses didn't intend to wait and find out. Neither did I. Nor did I fancy riding flat-out across ground pock-marked with gopher holes and badger burrows when there's a herd of charging musk oxen close behind me.

Our horses can easily outrun a musk ox. That was never a concern to me. I was concerned about holes, some of them almost impossible to see in the tall grass, yet potentially lethal if a horse stepped in one. I'd seen what the musk oxen did to my cap the day it blew off. That alone was reason enough to choose Eldorado over Fantasy.

I was about to ride from the yard when Couffer handed me his walkie-talkie. "Here. Take this. Call me when you've located the musk oxen." But a second later movie stock-supplier John Scott, sounding worried, called.

"Wait a minute, Mary. What about your horse? Is he liable to spook if you use it? Some horses do, you know. If you've never used one you'd better try it before you leave the yard." There was a brief pause. "*Have* you ever used one?"

I hadn't. "No, but I don't think it will bother him." And it didn't. A moment later, hearing a strange voice booming out of the air inches from his ears didn't even make Eldorado look surprised. Scott moved closer and gave my little Arabian an approving pat.

The musk oxen were so well hidden in a thick poplar bluff that it took a lot of riding to locate them. I might not have found them then if I hadn't caught a whiff of the peculiar male odour unique to bulls approaching rut. But now, having located the herd, I rode off some distance before calling Couffer, waiting back at the ranch buildings, to tell him which bush they were in and its relation to the blind. Almost immediately a thunderous voice came booming out of the walkie-talkie. "Good work, Mary! Do you think you can you keep them where they are until we get there?"

"I don't know." My hiss was a sibilant whisper. "Kivy's heard you and she's coming out of the bush right now. If she comes one step closer I'm leaving. And if you have anything more to say to me, don't shout. Whisper."

A minute later the faintest of whispers reached my years. "Well done, Mary. And thank you."

Then it hit me. I had given orders to a Hollywood VIP and he had thanked me. Yikes!

Although my riding cut down considerably on the amount of walking Clarence did each day, I still worried. What if one of the bulls should suddenly get upset at having so many strangers in his territory and see my husband as a threat to his harem? The hunters had spent months training for what they were doing, yet I'd heard one of them say to his companions, "I hope you have your life insurance in order."

I felt somewhat better when Clarence agreed there should be three riders in the area when filming was in progress. I expected that was mainly to quieten my fears, not because he felt there was any real danger. But that didn't matter; I'd be there on Eldorado with the walkie-talkie. If those at the blind saw potential trouble building they were to immediately call me. Then I'd alert the other riders, and we'd all go charging in, whooping and hollering like over-zealous hockey parents at a championship play-off game, because if we didn't frighten the musk oxen into running away quickly, they were apt to attack us.

One of the riders was a movie man good with a rope. He rode Image, Terry Lee's well-trained Arabian stallion. She rode Image's son, Gango White Gold (GWG to his friends), a strong, well-muscled three-year-old not so well trained, but already showing lots of promise as a stock horse.

Although our adrenalin never completely switched off, none of us were sorry when we had nothing to do but sit and swat mosquitoes off ourselves and our horses.

Having the movie makers on the ranch was a fascinating experience. I had good rapport with Jack Couffer's "woman" from Kenya. She keeps cheetahs and tigers as house pets, so is hardly a stranger to dangerous and exotic animals, yet she found the musk oxen "absolutely fascinating."

She told me later, "I was so thrilled at the wonderful close-ups the cameras were getting I didn't want to move, not even to brush off the horsefly that was biting my arm in case it scared the musk oxen." (Now, that's stoicism! An uninterrupted horsefly's bite is torture. It has jaws like steel-nosed pincers.)

"Then when the biggest bull swaggered up to the blind as if considering it for immediate demolition I can tell you everyone inside the blind was stiff with fright until your husband came and called him away. It's utterly amazing the way they listen to him. I'm so glad Jack let me go with him, because I had no idea musk oxen are such splendid animals. They look so magnificently wild and dangerous, yet they respond to your husband like well-trained dogs. It's no wonder Jack is so impressed with them. He says yours are by far the best-looking musk oxen he has ever seen, either in the wild or in captivity."

The child actor in the movie "Clan of the Cave Bear" was so terrified of the hunters his part had to be cut from the script. The Degenhardt youngsters and their cousin quickly became good friends with Keith Wardlow who played the part of Crug. From left to right, the children are Rory and Kerry Degenhardt, Bridget Currier, and little Heather Degenhardt.

This was the same lady who told me my grandchildren Kerry, Rory, and Heather Janine Degenhardt had taken her on a guided tour of the farmyard, with a running commentary about their cats, dogs, ponies, and even the garden and some of the plants in it. "They kept me so well entertained I didn't really mind when Jack said I couldn't go to the filming site with you in your truck that first evening. You know something else, Mrs. Burpee? I don't normally like other people's children. Actually, I think most of them are horrible little monsters, but I like your grandchildren. They are all so very special."

Well, I liked her too. She was a smart lady.

The day "Hollywood" returned to their mountaintop "location" near Penticton, B.C., most of them came to tell us they had enjoyed their time on the ranch. I too had mixed feelings about saying goodbye. Having a bit of Hollywood on the ranch had been mostly a fun experience, certainly different from anything we had ever done before. The musk oxen had justified my husband's faith in them, they had behaved well, and no one had been hurt.

During our Hollywood interlude our horses won respect for their breed from quarter-horse admirers who normally think of Arabians as millionaires' show pieces. And the copper-chestnut gelding who had once seemed "the chick too late out of its shell" had wound himself a little more tightly around my heart.

Chapter Fifteen

Miasma Success

It was that comfortable twilight zone when one is awake yet not quite ready to crawl out of a snug cocoon to face the challenges of a new day. But when the strident ringing of the phone shattered the morning silence, I was out of bed like a spring-released jack-in-the-box.

I lifted the receiver to hear "Hi, Mom. We're taking the horses to Rocky Ridges this morning. One of the bulls has a breeding problem so we have to split up his cows and put them in with the bulls in two other pastures. D'you want to come?" We had kept Rocky Ridges for pasture and crop land, after we moved to Gango Ranch.

"Sure thing, Terry Lee. How soon are you leaving?"

"Just as soon as Keith gets the stock trailer hooked up and Bob has Saucy saddled. I already have GWG in the barn. Fantasy too. I didn't think you'd want to miss a chance to ride at Rocky Ridges." Terry Lee knows her mother well.

"Great. Give me a few minutes to grab a bite to eat and I'll be right over. How long do you expect we'll be gone?"

"If we have good luck finding the herd and matching up the cow-calf pairs we should be finished by noon. But with cows you never know."

Ten minutes later I had grabbed my jacket off its peg and was heading out the door. The morning promised to be hot, but I've been a ranch wife too many years not to know a job that "shouldn't take long" could take all day. I also know that Alberta weather can change faster than a baseball coach can spit.

191

With three riders cutting and holding, and Keith on foot reading ear-tag numbers, it was relatively easy to identify cow-calf pairs and get them into two separate groups. The first group of animals had already gone to their new pasture.

We were riding back to move the second herd, a herd that included a cow with a lame calf, when Terry Lee looked at my little Arabian mare and then turned to Bob, who like most cowboys thought quarter-horses were needed for cattle work. "Bob, wouldn't you say that my Mom's eighteen-year-old Fantasy is still an amazingly good stock horse?"

Bob grunted a grudging "Yeah, I guess so."

I grinned and patted a silver-white neck shining with a prismatic sheen, murmuring, "If she'd nip the cows, instead of just threatening them, she'd be even better."

Terry Lee laughed. "But when she lays her ears flat back and swings her neck like a striking rattlesnake she looks fierce enough to scare most anything."

"Yeah, I know. She might look more dangerous than a cranky old gander but her threats are just bluff. She hasn't a mean hair on her and most of the cows know it."

Having said that, my thoughts went back to the spring cattle drive that had turned unbearably hot. The sun had beaten down on us like hammer strokes, cows still not fully shed out were slow and getting slower. Fantasy never blinked when the long willow switch I carried darted out past her face to swat some lagging critter. She knew willow switches and stock whips were meant for cows, not horses.

However, later that day Fantasy hadn't responded quite as quickly as I had wanted to speed up a dawdling heifer so she got a light swat on the rump with my stick. Her only reaction to that was to half turn her head and toss it as if saying, "Hey! Watch what you're doing. That was me you just hit."

When I swatted her again she flattened her ears, swished her tail, and glared back at me, but still didn't move any faster. So I swatted her a third time. That made her hump her back and give a few angry crow-hops. I couldn't let her get away with that sort of behaviour, so she got a harder swat.... It was then she realized that perhaps I hadn't been hitting her by mistake, I must want something. So she moved faster. She was an animal who aimed to please ... when she knew what was expected of her.

I patted her neck. Eighteen years old and never been swatted. Not many horses can claim that sort of distinction.

When we riders got to where Keith was waiting for us beside the crew-cab and stock trailer, Terry Lee asked, "Wouldn't it save time if Mom and I cut out the cow with the lame calf right here? We can take them back to the corrals while you and Bob are moving the rest of the herd to their pasture."

"Good idea. If I let down the fence in this corner you can take them through right here. No sense making the calf walk all the way back to the gate." Keith was pulling wires aside as he finished speaking.

With the cow and calf well started away from a herd already moving off in the opposite direction, we didn't anticipate any trouble. But that changed quickly when the cow looked back with a startled expression that seemed to translate into "Hot diggety! They're not leaving without me!" and went streaking after the disappearing herd, bellowing "Hey! Wait up, girls. I'm coming too."

While the horses were changing her mind on that score, the calf got himself badly tangled in the barbed wire Keith had thrown on the ground. Instead of lifting his foot so the wire could drop off, he went racing across the field bawling bloody mayhem and dragging thirty feet of fencing behind him. He very nearly got GWG tangled in barbed wire too.

When we had the wire problem beaten and the cow alongside her calf again he suddenly remembered to be lame. Fantasy had to almost push him now to keep him hobbling along behind his mother. "Too bad he couldn't have done all that running in the right direction," I snorted.

Terry Lee wore a disgusted look. "The way he was tearing around back there who'd ever guess he was lame?"

About this time the cow decided to rejoin her friends again. GWG had to do some fancy footwork to change her mind. Only she hadn't really changed it. She was just being cagey.

The next time she raced away we both went after her. There was no need for me to stay with the calf; he wasn't going anywhere. He'd be glad to flop down right where he was for a rest. He'd been trying to do just that for quite some time.

Thinking that was a mistake.

By the time we had the cow back to where her offspring should have been, there was no calf. He had utterly and completely vanished.

"Damn! If he sneaked into that poplar bluff and is lying down in there we'll have the devil's own time finding him. The underbrush is thicker than a musk oxen's winter coat.

"Fantasy can squeeze between the trees easier than GWG. Why don't you stay on the outside and stop the cow from trying to run back again while I locate the little cuss. He can't have gone far."

Once inside the bush I realized if I wanted to make any progress I had better get off and walk. That way, and with the mare following me, I was able to squeeze through narrower spaces, duck under lower branches, scramble more easily over tangled piles of half-rotten logs, or fight my way around wind-felled trees leaning like drunken revellers propped up by their more sober companions.

And to Terry Lee's anxious calls, "Can you see him yet?" the answer was always "No."

Finally one of us had a brain wave. Why not drive the cow into the grove of poplars, and let her find the calf? She'd know where it was. Then we'd get them both out of the bush and be on our way again. It sounded simple. Why hadn't we thought of it sooner?

The cow found her calf. She went directly to it. At least that part of our assumption proved correct. I got the pair started out of the bush, then had to yell to Terry Lee, "Ride around to the west side. It's so thick in here I've lost sight of them, but it sounds as if they're moving west."

Fantasy was so glad when she saw the edge of the bush just ahead that she could hardly wait for me to climb back on. Almost before I had, Terry Lee was calling, "Hey, Mom! Where's the calf?"

"Didn't it follow the cow out?" I felt as wilted as month-old lettuce. I'd have to go back into that damn bush again. But before I did the cow was off at a high-tailed gallop. I went to help bring her back.

This time when we had her heading in the right direction, I growled, "If the old stinker likes running so much why don't we keep her crowded between the horses and maybe we can gallop her all the way back to the corrals? We'll worry about the calf after we've got her penned up."

Actually I wasn't at all sure my suggestion would work. I've raced alongside more than one ornery critter, swatting it in the face hoping to make it turn, without much success. What about this cow? Would she turn ornery and charge one of our horses? If she did she had the weight to lift it off its feet and toss it out of her way. A cattle beast really on the prod will crash into most anything blocking its escape route. So far this cow hadn't done that. But would our luck hold?

It did.

When Terry Lee slammed the corral gate shut behind the cow, a little grin took over her face. "We should've done that in the first place, Mom. Keith and Bob should be back any minute. Bob has a rope. If he catches the calf we can load it into the trailer right where it is."

It sounded easy. Too easy.

We met the men just as we reached the bush. They were surprised to hear we'd had trouble. Everything had seemed to be going so well.

Terry Lee agreed to stay on the outside with the three horses and yell if she saw the calf come out. The rest of us split up, each taking different directions through the tangled undergrowth. Getting snagged, zapped, tripped, and scratched made one wonder what we saw in rural life. But it could have been worse. Nobody stumbled into a hornets' nest.

Finally Keith sang out, "I see him. He's heading west. Can you see him, Bob?"

"Naw. I can't see nuthin'!"

Now I was yelling. "He's over here. I'll head him towards you, Bob."

There was the sound of bodies crashing through underbrush, followed by an impatient "Have you got a rope on him yet, Bob?"

"Hell, no! Can't swing a rope for trees."

"Can you sneak up and drop it over his head?"

Bob's answer to that blistered the air for quite a while with colour *and* originality.

Meantime the calf had disappeared again. No one could see him.

Finally Keith's voice rang out. "He's over here. Heading east. On the run. He'll be out in the open in a minute. Terry Lee, quick! Ride around there. Try to hold him where Bob has some hope of roping him."

I half-raced, half-stumbled out of the bush and grabbed Fantasy from Terry Lee, who was just galloping up. The calf, which had been hobbling like a cripple on one crutch, was streaking away now like a young Donovan Bailey. Terry Lee jabbed her heels into GWG, and I followed on Fantasy. But Bob's roping horse, Saucy, which Terry Lee had let go thinking he would follow the other horses, went trotting gaily off towards the corrals, leaving Bob on foot and limping.

The calf wasn't sticking around to be roped, but he was heading in the right direction, so we were making miles. But it didn't last. The calf ducked through a fence and raced towards another herd of cows. No problem. We'd haze that herd to the corrals, cut out the calf, then bring the rest back.

And it would have worked if the calf hadn't developed a violent thirst at the precise moment the herd was skirting a muskeg-rimmed dugout. Calves could step from one undulating hummock to another without breaking through. Horses couldn't. They'd sink in up to their fetlocks, or beyond.

So there was nothing for it but to wait for him to drink his fill with whatever patience we could muster, but when he moved farther out into the muskeg and stood there as if he planned to stay for quite some time, patience vanished.

Yet we couldn't risk getting the horses hopelessly mired. So we began exercising vocal cords and throwing sticks and clods. That finally prompted the calf to move to a hummocky area that might bear a man's weight, if he was cautious. But it wasn't easy for Bob to throw a lasso while balancing on two tufts of grass that shook and quivered like soft Jell-O. It seemed the calf had us stumped.

That's when Keith, looking as if his sense of humour had deserted him, growled, "Bob, throw me the rope. I'm going in after the little bugger."

He grabbed the rope, yanked his shirt open, and tossed it and his boots to one side. That made sense. No need to get all his clothes muddy. But when he unzipped his pants and shucked out of them I wondered where I'd look if his shorts were added to the pile.

A determined glitter darkened his eyes as he waded out into the ooze in nothing but socks and shorts. I had to stifle a naughty giggle.

The calf took one look at Keith and lit out in a panic, half swimming, half wallowing towards Bob. Keith flung the rope to Bob, who in reaching for it floundered off his hummock, and that startled the calf into heading back towards Keith. Only now Keith didn't have a rope.

But Dr. Keith Degenhardt isn't one to give up on any job before he's given it his best shot. He hurled himself at the calf in a tackle that would have done a football player proud. A tackle that brought a startled gasp from his wife. "Keith! What on earth do you think you're doing?" But when he went down he had his arms firmly around the calf's middle.

Man and calf floundered and fought, dragging each other deeper and deeper into the muskeg. When they finally re-surfaced they were so covered in mud and slime and green ooze they looked like pigs coming out of a hog-wallow. The calf, scared half out of its wits, was too slippery for Keith to hang onto now and it broke away. Too frightened to look where it was going, it was running in a bee-line straight towards Bob. For a moment it looked as if the two might collide. Then Bob made a good throw and a cheer went up.

Terry Lee and GWG dragged the calf, bellowing but still fighting, to the stock trailer and Bob shoved him in, while Keith cleaned the mud off his glasses and from around his eyes as best he could. When he could see again he gave a dismal grin. "I'd better leave my clothes off until I get showered."

Back at the corrals with the cow, calf, and horses in the stock trailer, everyone but Keith headed for the back seat of the crew-cab. Keith shot us a mischievous over-the-shoulder grin as he eased in behind the wheel. "My, my! Isn't it strange how no one wants to sit beside me today." Terry Lee gave him a weak smile, then turned to me with an anxious look. "I hope you're not too hungry, Mom."

I shook my head, then glanced at my watch. It was after 3 o'clock.

Chapter Sixteen

Horse Sense

"It's *okay*, Ed. I had intended riding this morning anyway, so I might just as well ride around your wheat field. If I see Julson's cattle in there I'll drive them out for you. Except the beggars aren't likely to stay out, you know. A cow doesn't have to be 'breechy' to step over his fences. They're all so dilapidated."

"Yeah, I know. He hasn't anything that remotely resembles a decent fence on the place. But if they are in my crop and you can get them out I'd sure appreciate it. Maybe the next time the buggers get out, the devil will send them in a different direction." Ed Southoff grinned facetiously as he walked back to his pick-up truck.

Julson was known to be mentally challenged (his mother blamed it on having fallen on his head as a baby), so perhaps that's why he didn't have a decent fence on his farm. On the other hand, maybe he was smarter than the neighbours thought and didn't want good fences. Without them his cows would never be short of pasture, but could grow fatter than ten-year-old hogs, grazing roadside ditches and any of his neighbours' crops that took their fancy. So no wonder some folks whispered that Julson wasn't nearly as short-changed in the mentality department as he liked to let on.

Soon after Ed Southoff had left I was riding Fantasy, an Arabian mare who rarely shied, around the edges of his wheat field, checking out every poplar bush I came to for stray cattle. I was circling the last bush when, without any warning, Fantasy shied so unexpectedly and so violently I very nearly flew off. I stayed on but the saddle horn hit my right hand such a whack that at first I was

201

sure my thumb must be broken. (It hurt so much that later in the day Clarence drove me 40 miles to have it X-rayed. It wasn't broken. Only badly bruised.)

It took a lot of urging to get Fantasy to re-approach the bush but I needed to check it out more closely. I was sure it must have been Julson's cattle that had startled my horse. If they were lying down she might have heard but not seen them, but even so, what was there about that to make her shy so violently? And why was she still acting so frightened, so obviously scared to go anywhere near the bush? It didn't make any sense for a good stock horse to suddenly behave as if cows were aliens from outer space. Then, as a memory clicked, I grinned and patted Fantasy's neck.

When anyone confronts Julson about the way his cattle are constantly getting out, making a nuisance of themselves in the neighbours' grain fields, hopeless despair is written in every line of his drooping shoulders. His unwashed clothes hang from his sagging frame like broken wings on a raven, he wrings his hands together as if deeply hurt that the matter has been taken so completely out of his control, then moistens his lips and says in a deadpan voice, "It's the devil that makes them do it."

So? Was it Julson's devil that had spooked my horse? It certainly wasn't his cows. They weren't in the bush, nor could I see anything else that should have frightened her.

Yet on the ride home Fantasy stayed as tense and edgy as a cornered wolverine, and it got worse each time we approached a poplar bluff. Nor did it end there. For the rest of the summer she acted scared every time we neared a grove of poplars. At the time I supposed her unusual behaviour meant she must have smelled a bear or perhaps even a cougar. There were reports that both had been seen in the district. Yet several years later I began wondering if it could have been something far more grisly.

A local man had vanished somewhat mysteriously, but as he was alleged to have been involved in drug smuggling it was generally believed he had skipped the country to escape arrest. The police had dragged a near-by lake for a body, but had found nothing. Which only bolstered the commonly held belief that the missing man had "done a flit," especially as over the years numerous reports filtered back to the district that he had been seen in faraway places.

So years later a chilling jolt ran up my spine when the story leaked out that a deer hunter had stumbled on what turned out to be part of a human skull. It was found close to the bush where Fantasy had shied that day at Julson's non-existent cows. The skull, which the police believed belonged to the missing man, had a bullet hole in it which they said suggested suicide. Yet the man's family said "no way." He wasn't suicidal when he came to say goodbye, but he was nervous. As if there was a need to get away quickly.

An extensive police search with dogs and metal detectors in the area where the skull fragment was found didn't reveal either a human skeleton or a weapon, but they hadn't gone into the bush Fantasy had shied at. They did after I told them my story, and they did find bones, but they were the bones of some long-dead animal, not of a human. Nor was any weapon ever reported found. So had there been a suicide? Or a murder? And had Fantasy somehow sensed it?

Or had it happened miles away and coyotes had carried the skull-fragment onto the Southoff land? Perhaps eventually someone will stumble onto a piece of evidence that will answer those questions. Until that happens I only know it had to have been something unusual to spook my little grey Arabian. Julson would probably have wagged his head and muttered dolefully, "The devil made her do it!"

Devil or not, now when the Arabian I'm riding snorts and tenses up, I may not see or smell what it does but I'm prepared to believe it is telling me there is something unusual in the vicinity.

Actually, I had been counting on that ability to detect the unusual the day I had ridden Khem slowly along little-used roads adjacent to Hughenden, and to our farm.

A fifteen-year-old boy was missing from school. No one knew what had happened to him, except that, unknown to his parents, he had been skipping school a lot recently with the school bully, a much bigger and older boy who wasn't considered too bright in the head. Yet this time the bully swore he knew nothing about the younger lad's sudden disappearance from school. When they were notified the boy's parents were frantic.

To be doing something, anything that might help, I saddled Khem and rode the side roads, counting on the stallion to snort and let me know if he sensed anything unusual in the trail-bordering bushes. Although I stayed as tense as a starving cat at a mouse hole throughout the entire ride, Khem never snorted nor shied, for there was no body. The boy had thumbed a ride out of town and was into Saskatchewan by the time school was out and he was reported missing. Fortunately that story had a happy ending.

We never used to see ravens in our part of Alberta. So the winter we heard and saw the first raven it came as a surprise. An even bigger surprise was the way the horses reacted when they heard its croaky caw. They stood as a group, heads up, ears pricked, watching and listening to it as if asking themselves, "What's that dumb crow doing back here this early? It isn't spring yet."

They acted in a similar fashion the day a colourful flotilla of hot air balloons from Calgary went sailing over our farm. We humans were outside admiring the balloons' colourful designs, waving to the people in their baskets, and speculating on where they were going, when we noticed the horses were watching them too. When the balloons floated off to the east the horses galloped to the highest hill in their pasture and stood watching them even after they had disappeared from our sight.

I don't normally wear shorts, especially not around the horses. So the July day I walked down to see them while wearing shorts their heads flew up and they stared at me. Even my mare seemed on the verge of turning to race away from this strange-looking critter with the long skinny legs until I spoke to her. Then she nickered and came to me. The same thing has happened if I'm wearing something brightly coloured, or noticeably different from what they are used to seeing me in.

The time a construction crew was putting up a big power installation in a corner of what had been our land Fantasy was convinced there was something so very wrong about what they were doing that she wouldn't pass the place where the men were working. I had to get off and lead her by it, and even then she was so nervous and jittery it was as if she expected to be momentarily blasted into outer space.

On another occasion, by paying attention to what the horses were trying to tell us we saved a valuable filly from being stolen and taken out of the country.

It was that time in a late winter afternoon when the world seems to hang a few moments between reality and myth, yet the horses were galloping about as if they were very perturbed. When I went out to find out why, I discovered a yearling filly was missing. The horses seemed to be trying to lead me to that part of their pasture that couldn't be seen from the house. Peering through the encroaching dusk I was sure there were tracks leading straight across what should have been an unbroken expanse of snow in the adjacent field. But why would the filly, even if she had somehow gotten over the fence, run away from the other horses like that? She should be right there waiting to be let back in with them, yet she wasn't. It didn't make sense.

Logic and apprehension began jockeying for position in my mind. My nerve endings were already sending out warning signals that something about this didn't look right, so apprehension won easily when I got to the gate and saw the imprints of a man's boots in the snow. The tracks of a second horse, and a discarded pail still containing a few oats, fleshed out the story. Our filly had been stolen. And I intended to find her.

Hurrying to the house I met Clarence just as he got back from doing the cattle chores. As I fixed his supper (a brittle diabetic needs to eat at regular intervals), I filled him in on what I had seen. As I pulled on snow boots and warmer clothes he phoned the police to tell them we suspected a horse-mad teenager had stolen a valuable filly out of our pasture and that Clarence would meet them at the boy's place in an hour. Meantime I would follow the tracks in the snow to be sure where they went, and if the filly was there, as we expected, I'd have her haltered and in the yard by the time the police and Clarence got there. The forecast was for snow and wind before morning and I wanted to make sure I got to the filly before snow obliterated her tracks.

My boots made loud crunching sounds as I slogged steadily through the crusted drifts. Stars in a midnight-blue sky glittered feverishly as if trying to compete with the silvery light of a full moon that made it easy to follow the filly's tracks.

When I got to the boy's house and knocked on the door, his mother said he wasn't home. When I told her I had come to get the filly he had taken from our pasture, she denied he had done any such thing. When I said I had followed the tracks, seen the filly in their pasture—in the moonlight it had been easy to spot an Arabian in a herd of scrub animals—she still insisted it was their filly I had seen, the one her son was taking to Saskatchewan just as soon as he got their half-ton gassed up and borrowed some stock-racks.

She was still swearing her son's innocence when I walked into the pasture and called to the filly, who immediately trotted over to me. I had the young mare haltered and back in the boy's yard by the time the police and Clarence drove up. They were followed seconds afterwards by a fifteen-year-old, who was illegally driving his Dad's half-ton truck, with the borrowed stock-racks already in place.

Storm clouds were now thudding steadily across the western sky, obliterating some of the stars, and the moon had lost its lustre. The wind was rising to a mournful wail. Before morning the world would have a fresh blanket of fluffy white snow. Tracking the filly then would have been impossible.

Had I ignored what the horses had been trying to tell me that evening, and been even half an hour later in getting to the filly, she would have been out of the country and we might never have seen her again. It was a sobering thought.

Because the boy was under age he was never charged with theft, but there were no tears shed in the community when he and his transient family moved to another district.

Chapter Seventeen

October

October is painting the countryside with a splendour no artist's brush can ever duplicate. October. Indian summer in all its glory. My favourite time to ride.

I saddle Fantasy and head past the corral that once was home to Khem, a horse that made dreams come true. It seems a long time since his eager whinny reached out to welcome me. His corral is silent. It's empty now.

Nearing the new ranch house (home to Terry Lee, her husband Keith, and their three children), Fantasy sidesteps like a skittish three-year-old, her nostrils flaring, her eyes wide. There is something about kids bouncing on a trampoline that affects her that way.

The grandchildren. Already in their teens. A time to metamorphose from the sheltered chrysalis of childhood into an adult world. A world of temptations, decisions, and challenge. And sometimes heartbreak.

The Terrible Teens. Are they really so terrible? They weren't for us. Our children's venture into adulthood was a time of camaraderie, of shared ideas, opinions, goals, confidences.

There were no arguing or shouting matches. Heather, knowing how it was among her classmates, came to me one afternoon puzzling over why we were different. "Mom, Sandra and her mother had another big fight last night. She says they are always arguing and screaming at each other, and that all girls and their mothers fight a lot."

"Oh." It wasn't quite a question.

There was a thoughtful silence for a moment, and when Heather spoke again she sounded as if there was something bothering her she hadn't quite been able to lay her finger on. "We don't fight, do we, Mom?"

To my smiled "No I guess we don't," she added as if with sudden enlightenment, "You tell me what you think I should do and I do it." I wasn't sure if that was a compliment, or the reverse.

Then, as if having said her say and the matter was now settled, Heather headed for the door, calling back over her shoulder, "Terry Lee and I are going to ride down to see the beaver dam. Want to come?"

"*Okay*. But first I have to finish this casserole for supper. You girls go ahead. I'll catch up." Riding was our time for discussions and shared confidences. It was a time I valued a lot. I think our children did too.

I supposed Clarence and I were normal parents, no better, no worse than average, so how was it that we were actually enjoying this phase of our children's lives? The so-called 'terrible teens.'

Then it hit me. It was the horses.

Our children each had an Arabian mare of their own to love, train, and be proud of. Having a horse entwined around their hearts, its care and progress their responsibility, must have been, without our knowing it, the secret formula.

Past the trampoline Fantasy breaks into a mile-eating trot. I see the silver sheen of her coat reflected briefly in the window of the house where Clarence and I have lived since Terry Lee and her husband Keith decided it was time to put their varied agriculture degrees to practical use.

The flowers around the house are all gone now, but towering evergreens make a magnificent backdrop for the display of fall colours flaunted by native poplars, planted birch and tamarack. And near the house is an Ontario oak. Small yet, but it's working on it.

Fantasy seems to read my mind. She turns the corner and heads east as if knowing instinctively that today we are heading for a hill so high it gives a breathtaking view of the surrounding countryside for miles in every direction. Dust rises from the flashing hooves in smoking clouds of grey. If a car should pass us now, both horse and rider will be enveloped in a swirling fog of dust, but this is a little-used dirt road. There's not likely to be any traffic today.

There's the musk ox pasture with its link-wire fence and many memories. But no musk oxen are in it now. There haven't been for several years. It's an ideal place for horses. Yet today I see only bulls ... bulls waiting for next year's breeding season. And of course the deer. There are always deer in the musk ox pasture. They feel safe there.

Another mile and Fantasy climbs sharply. My ears don't pop today. Sometimes they do. The mare stops, fidgeting, eager to get going again. But soon something about the place, its peace and splendour, touch her too and she stands quietly, her dark eyes gazing off into the distance. Then she drops her head to the alfalfa, still not frozen, growing at her feet and she begins to eat. My eyes too are sweeping the distance, taking a memory photo of the panorama that stretches away on every side. The words of my favourite hymn, *My God How Great Thou Art*, strum through my mind. The man who wrote those words must have known just such a spot as this.

The high dome of heaven is scratched with a myriad of pencil-thin lines as Canada geese vee their way southward. Will they land on Shorncliff lake? The lake I used to sail on with my Dad in the *Bellkenna*, a sailboat he owned jointly with Ed Bell, the Ford car dealer. Today the lake's calm reflections make it look almost too close for the two miles I know it to be, but the answer is still "no." The geese are flying too high. They won't land there. They must be heading for lakes farther south. I can just make out one lying snug against the horizon, twinkling in the sunlight like a diamond bracelet on a wrist. It must be Houcher Lake. Most days it's hidden by the blue of distance. But this afternoon the air is clear and sparkling as mountain dew. And a new moon is already in the sky.

Is it still the harvest moon? How many times have I ridden Pompey under a great silver orb that had the witchery to turn an ordinary balmy prairie night into a magical, mysterious place? A tropical island where poplars became transformed into softly waving palm trees and the wind soughing through their branches became the gentle lapping of an ocean on its sandy shore.

That seems only a nebulous memory now.

Away to the north is the farm where I was born. The farm where my love of horses took root and flourished. The trees Mom had us plant to commemorate a King's coronation so long ago still identify the place. British royalty always meant a lot to Mom. And why not? Her father's uncle was a friend (and advisor too, they say) of Queen Victoria.

Where once freshly threshed straw-stacks dotted the landscape, stacks for children to climb up and pigs to burrow under, I now see tiny black machines looking like miniature match-stick toys being pushed across a table-top. Men are hurrying to get the big round straw-bales off their fields so they can get the cattle moved onto them, others are rushing to get more fall cultivating done before freeze-up shuts them down.

A quarter turn and a small figure gallops over a distant ridge. I know immediately it is Liz, a young woman who is a kindred spirit in our love of horses. She rides a Gango Arabian.

That steers my thoughts to other people, people scattered throughout Canada and Alaska. We may have met briefly, or not at all, but we exchange letters and have a rather special friendship because in horses we share a common bond. What could be more rewarding to a breeder than knowing her stock is bringing happiness to so many other people?

I swing around. To the west the Gango Ranch buildings show dark against the sun. A wave of nostalgia sweeps over me. That place represents 43 years of working together with the man of my choice to make it what it is. They were busy years, challenging years. But they were happy too. Always some new goal to work towards.

I think of my husband, the tall, quiet, handsome man my parents once thought would get short shrift because he didn't ride a horse ... except the time he and I rode Pompey halterless in from the pasture. A man who never doubted dreams can come true, if you work at them.

Always so calm, so patient, so reassuring. Always there when I needed him most. But not now. Strokes left him paralyzed, unable to walk. Even talking was an effort. So was eating. Yet he rarely complained. Now he is gone. And I can't honestly wish him back. For he is at peace.

I turn Fantasy and head back towards my empty house. The house may look empty, but it isn't. Not really. It's peopled with so many good memories that I can never feel really lonely there.

Nor is the pasture empty. It too has its good memories, but it also has its flesh and blood. As I ride closer a whinny reaches out to me from among the horses grazing there. One horse has flung up her head to watch, then trots briskly towards the gate. It's Olympus God-dess, Khem's final gift to me. She is waiting.

Someday Fantasy, already nearing 20, will get too old for long hours under saddle, then Goddess will step in to take her mother's place among the horses around my heart.

It is October. Such a lot has changed since that April springtime so long ago when Darky outran the stork. But not my love of horses. When my November and December beckon I hope I'll see them through with horses still entwined around my heart.

I pat Fantasy, turn her into the pasture, watch as she rolls three times, shakes the dust from her coat. Then, frisking and cavorting, she and her daughter gallop away to join their pasture mates. I turn and walk slowly away.

Mary Kennedy and Pompey, Vincent Cole and Paddy.

Armloads of kittens. Eileen and Barbe Kennedy.
Paddy looks bored.

Left to right: Alex Allan on his horse, Eileen Kennedy,
Mary on Pompey, Everett Moore standing.

Pompey and three sisters. Eileen, Barbara and Mary.

Three good friends. Mary, Pompey and Sniffer.

Pompey and Mary ready for a winter gallop.

Pompey and Mary Kennedy. It was hard to know who owned them.

Look, no hands! Left to right, Everett Moore, Lois Kreisz, Alex Allan, Mary Kennedy, Mike Kreisz and Barbe Kennedy on Mike's horse.

Sniffer gets a ride on Barbe's pony Topsy, while Eileen smiles approval.

Pompey and Mary and a friend.

Getting the herd ready for the long move to Rocky Ridges.

Heather loves riding Nifty.

Terry Lee rides Khem's daughter,
Gango Desert Song for the first time.

Terry Lee and Firefly.

Khem moving a small herd of cows from stand of Russian Wild Rye planted in rows for seed production.

Look! No feet on the ground. Tery lee at the halter.

This picture shows Khem's blind side.

Is the cow calving over there going to need help?

Do you see any more over there?

Rod Burpee with Nat. Terry Lee on Butterfly, the author on Khem.

Quit scolding. I am standing still.

Now come on. let's get going.

Our cattle drives have always been family affairs. Riders from left to right, Terry Lee on Firefly, Rod on Eldorado, Mary on Khem.

When on a cattle-drive the cows bunched into a jostling mass, it helped if a rider split the herd giving the animals at the rear more space and something to follow.

One-year-old Kerry Degenhardt and his mother's range stallion,
Gango Raffles Image.

Terry Lee trains Firefly's son, Gango Raffles Image

*Terry Lee Burpee on Gango Firefly. It's a chilly spring
morning but we'll ride anyway.*

Firefly gets her hooves trimmed. It's easier if Terry Lee sits.

Firefly, one of the proud breed.

Grandkids Michael Lea and Heather Degenhardt on a couple of old mares, Sha-Em and Topsey.

This little rascal will try almost anything to get his mother up to feed him, but that is something Sha-Em will do when she is ready.

Heather Burpee on Sha-Em.

Three Burpee kids. Left to right, Rod on the Mexican burro Perky who doesn't have power steering. Heather on Shasta who does, and Terry Lee on Pablo's daughter, Butterfly.

Good reflections. Rod tries out the boat he built while Grannie and Granpa Kennedy, Mary and Heather Burpee stand and watch. His sister Terry Lee watches from Firefly's back.

Heather and Sha-Em waiting to ride in the Hardisty rodeo parade.

Heather Degenhardt at the halter of her Aunt Heather's mare Sha-Em. A stroke a year later claimed Sha-Ems life at the age of 38.

*Rod Burpee and one of the little Shetland foals. Heather with
Sha-Ems filly, Gango Shannondoah.*

Mandy, an Arab/Shetland pony was Rod's first 4-H horse.

A young visitor from Japan has his first-ever ride.
Eldorado doesn't mind.

This Shetland foal had an unfortunate encounter with a porcupine.
Terry Lee helps her Dad pull out the quills while Mary watches.

Rod and Eldorado ready for a winter ride.

Rod Burpee and the three-year-old Gango Desert Wings.

Rod on Eldorado and some of their 4-H friends.

Sacks are stuffed with hay. The back one was taken off before the picture was taken. The foal belongs to Butterfly, the pony Terry Lee rode for this excursion.

Summer trail riders. Left to right, Dorothy Allan, Eileen Kennedy, Barbara Kennedy, Margaret Wall, Mary Kennedy.

Lady carried a load of happiness. Left to right, Roderick Burpee and his cousins, Neil and Pattie Butchart.

Nanna, the Burpee children's eighty-year-old paternal grandmother was a brave lady. Here she is riding in the pony cart with Rod and the Shetland, Lady.

Rod uses Lady and the pony cart to haul greenfeed to the barn.

Winter trail riders on Gango Arabians.

Perky doesn't have power steering, but she is still fun to ride.

*Clarence and Rod check the stand of Russian Wild Rye
with Thimbles and the pony cart.*

Gango Arabians pasturing on Russian Wild Rye grass.

Two good friends.

AGMV Marquis

MEMBER OF SCABRINI MEDIA

Quebec, Canada
2004